Summary of Contents

FANCY FORM DESIGN

BY **JINA BOLTON**
TIM CONNELL
DEREK FEATHERSTONE

Fancy Form Design

by Jina Bolton, Tim Connell, and Derek Featherstone

Technical Editor: Raena Jackson Armitage   **Chief Technical Officer**: Kevin Yank

Editor: Kelly Steele   **Indexer**: Fred Brown

Managing Editor: Chris Wyness   **Cover Design**: Alex Walker

Reviewer: Avi Miller

Printing History:

First Edition: October 2009

Published by SitePoint Pty. Ltd.

48 Cambridge Street
Collingwood, Victoria, Australia 3066
Web: www.sitepoint.com
Email: business@sitepoint.com

ISBN 978-0-9805768-4-9
Printed and bound in Canada

About the Authors

Jina Bolton is a designer at Crush + Lovely in San Francisco and speaks at conferences around the world. She co-authored *The Art and Science of CSS* (Melbourne: SitePoint, 2007) and has also written articles for web industry-related publications. Jina digs sushi and robots—so you'll find her at http://sushiandrobots.com.

Tim Connell lives and breathes the Web and can often be found atop a soapbox talking about users, accessibility, and sexy techniques. Tim is a technical consultant for Squiz (http://squiz.net), a leading enterprise content management company, and a developer with Fresh Interface (http://freshinterface.net). Outside of the Web, Tim likes to enjoy good company at the local watering hole. Tim lives in Sydney, Australia.

Engaging, surprising, and inspiring, Derek Featherstone is an internationally known authority on accessibility and web development. As founder of Further Ahead (http://furtherahead.com), he has been a user experience and accessibility consultant in demand since 1999, and regularly wows audiences with practical demonstrations of creative solutions to accessibility issues. He is the Group Lead of the influential Web Standards Project and blogs at http://boxofchocolates.ca.

About the Technical Editor

Raena Jackson Armitage made her way to SitePoint via a circuitous route involving web development, training, and speaking. A lifelong Mac fangirl, she's written for *The Mac Observer* and *About This Particular Macintosh*. Raena loves knitting, reading, and riding her bike around Melbourne in search of the perfect all-day breakfast. Raena's personal web site is at http://raena.net.

About the Chief Technical Officer

As Chief Technical Officer for SitePoint, Kevin Yank oversees all of its technical publications—books, articles, newsletters, and blogs. He has written over 50 articles for SitePoint, but is best known for his book, *Build Your Own Database Driven Website Using PHP & MySQL*. Kevin lives in Melbourne, Australia, and enjoys performing improvised comedy theatre and flying light aircraft.

About SitePoint

SitePoint specializes in publishing fun, practical, and easy-to-understand content for web professionals. You can visit http://sitepoint.com to access our books, newsletters, articles, and community forums.

To God, first and foremost. To Jason, Dad, and the rest of my family. To my amazing friends both online and in "real life." To my co-workers at Crush + Lovely who have become great friends. I love you all so much.

—Jina

Thanks to all the top people in my life: there are many of you, and you know who you are.

—Tim

For my wife Kathryn, and our wonderful children Kaitlyn, Kyla, and Kampbell. Without you, none of this would matter.

—Derek

Table of Contents

Preface

Think about all the web sites you use each day. Perhaps you have a blog, or at least like to comment on blogs. You might use social networks like Facebook to keep in touch with friends, or a web-based email service like Yahoo or Google. Perhaps you have some favorite forums you like to visit, or a photo-sharing site where you can upload your happy snaps. Maybe you bought a product online recently, or reviewed one. What do all these activities have in common? Forms!

Every day, people use forms for all kinds of activities—they're some of the most interactive parts of any site. Effective, beautiful forms make for happy visitors who find it easy to interact with your site and come back for a second helping. Poorly designed forms annoy and frustrate users, and might even merit a quick trip to the browser's **Back** button.

Yet, despite their obvious importance and ubiquity, many web developers find the task of creating forms to be boring, difficult, frustrating, or time-consuming. The truth is that the secret to creating beautiful, user-friendly, engaging forms—and having a good time while you're at it—is no secret at all. Like everything else, it's easy once you know how.

This book is full of tips, techniques, and practical examples to help you build breathtaking, beautiful forms. We'll guide you through the whole process, from the initial research and planning stages, all the way through to designing, building, and enhancing your form.

By the time you reach the end of this book, you'll be able to jump into your next forms project with confidence. What's more, your forms will be more than just good—they'll be downright *fancy*.

Who Should Read This Book?

Perhaps you're an experienced web developer who's already built some forms, but found the results were less than ideal. Perhaps you're just starting out on your web development career. You might be an interface designer, a HTML and CSS coder, a JavaScript guru, or a bit of all three. If you're involved with any part of the form creation process, this book is for you.

What's Covered in This Book?

Chapter One: Planning

A great form must start with a great plan. We'll discuss some of the gadgets, widgets, and goodies that are available to you. Then, we'll examine how thorough research creates a strong foundation for your forms: use cases and scenarios, paper prototyping, visitor profiles, and more all come together to help you build a solid picture of what your forms ought to be like.

Chapter Two: Designing

Naturally, a beautiful visual design for your forms will wow your visitors. But a truly effective design is one that enhances usability as well as aesthetics. In this chapter, we examine how a grid system, color, typography, icons, and textures come together to create a pleasing and easy to use design for your forms.

Chapter Three: Structure

A strong skeleton for your form is essential, and that skeleton is made of semantic, structural HTML. We look into best-practice methods you can use today in your sites that emphasize usability, accessibility, and meaningful code.

Chapter Four: Styling

Veteran form developers can tell many a tale of browser bugs, strange inconsistencies, and irritating behavior. In this chapter we examine some proven CSS tricks and techniques for form layout that will mesh perfectly with our clean, semantic HTML, and match your form's design perfectly to the rest of your site.

Chapter Five: Enhancing

Careful use of JavaScript can make the difference between "Gee, that's a nice form," and "Wow, that's actually fun to use!" The techniques we describe in this chapter cover functional enhancements such as client-side validation and password strength testing, as well as aesthetic changes like customized pull-down menus and checkboxes.

The SitePoint Forums

The SitePoint Forums[1] are discussion forums where you can ask questions about anything related to web design, development, hosting, and online marketing. You may, of course, answer questions, too. That's how a discussion forum site works—some people ask, some people answer—and most people do a bit of both. Sharing your knowledge benefits others and strengthens the community. A lot of interesting and experienced web designers and developers hang out there. It's a good way to learn new stuff, have questions answered in a hurry, and just have fun.

The Design Your Site forum has subforums devoted to every facet of web design—HTML and CSS advice, graphics tips, accessibility and usability, and even site reviews and critiques.[2] It's free to sign up, and it takes just a few minutes.

This Book's Web Site

No book is perfect, and we expect that watchful readers will be able to spot at least one or two mistakes before the end of this one. The Errata page on the book's web site will always have the latest information about known typographical errors and updates. You'll find the book's web site at http://www.sitepoint.com/books/forms1/. If you find a problem, you'll also be able to report it here.

The SitePoint Newsletters

In addition to books like this one, SitePoint publishes free email newsletters, such as the *SitePoint Design View*, the *SitePoint Tribune*, and the *SitePoint Tech Times*, to name a few. In them, you'll read about the latest news, product releases, trends, tips, and techniques for all aspects of web development. Sign up to one or more SitePoint newsletters at http://www.sitepoint.com/newsletter/.

---

[1] http://www.sitepoint.com/forums/
[2] http://www.sitepoint.com/forums/forumdisplay.php?f=40

The SitePoint Podcast

Join the SitePoint Podcast team for news, interviews, opinion, and fresh thinking for web developers and designers. They discuss the latest web industry topics, present guest speakers, and interview some of the best minds in the industry. You can catch up on the latest and previous podcasts at http://www.sitepoint.com/podcast/ or subscribe via iTunes.

Your Feedback

If you're unable to find an answer through the forums, or if you wish to contact us for any other reason, the best place to write to is books@sitepoint.com. We have a well-staffed email support system set up to track your inquiries, and if our support team members are unable to answer your question, they'll send it straight to us. Suggestions for improvements, as well as notices of any mistakes you may find, are especially welcome.

Conventions Used in This Book

You'll notice that we've used certain typographic and layout styles throughout this book to signify different types of information. Look out for the following items:

Tips, Notes, and Warnings

 Hey, You!

Tips will give you helpful little pointers.

 Ahem, Excuse Me ...

Notes are useful asides that are related—but not critical—to the topic at hand. Think of them as extra tidbits of information.

 Make Sure You Always ...

... pay attention to these important points.

 Watch Out!

Warnings will highlight any gotchas that are likely to trip you up along the way.

Markup Samples

Any code—HTML, CSS, or JavaScript—will be displayed using a fixed-width font like so:

```
<h1>A perfect summer's day</h1>
<p>It was a lovely day for a walk in the park. The birds
were singing and the kids were all back at school.</p>
```

If the markup forms part of the book's code archive, the name of the file will appear at the top of the program listing, like this:

example.css

```
.footer {
  background-color: #CCC;
  border-top: 1px solid #333;
}
```

If only part of the file is displayed, this is indicated by the word *excerpt*:

example.css (excerpt)

```
  border-top: 1px solid #333;
```

If additional code is to be inserted into an existing example, the new code will be displayed in bold:

```
function animate() {
  new_variable = "Hello";
}
```

Also, where existing code is required for context, rather than repeat all the code, a vertical ellipsis will be displayed:

```
function animate() {
  ⋮
  return new_variable;
}
```

Some lines of code are intended to be entered on one line, but we've had to wrap them because of page constraints. A ➥ indicates a line break that exists for formatting purposes only, and should be ignored.

```
URL.open("http://www.sitepoint.com/blogs/2007/05/28/user-style-she
➥ets-come-of-age/");
```

Acknowledgements

Jina Bolton

Thank-you to the people of SitePoint for the opportunity to work on this book—particularly Raena who was patient, gave great feedback, and is also fun to follow on Twitter. Thanks to Derek for his expertise and for being a pleasure to work with. It's been an honor co-authoring a book with you. Thanks to Tim for helping shift this book out the door! Thanks to my co-workers at Crush + Lovely who have been amazing and understanding, and even gave me business hours to work on this book! And, of course, thanks to the rest of all my family and friends who have helped me along the way.

Tim Connell

Thank-you to my wonderful friends and family for all of your support and encouragement—especially to Mum, for being my mum; to Jerome, for making me smile and think at exactly the right moments; to Heather and Corine for being the most brilliant friends and business partners a guy could ask for, and to Squiz and the many inspirational people I work with. Thanks also to my amazing co-authors Derek and Jina; to Raena and the SitePoint crew; to Avi Miller for the feedback, and to everyone else who read, wrote, or pondered over the words in this book.

Derek Featherstone

First and foremost, thank-you to all of my family for accepting my geekiness and my love for the Web and trying to make it a better place. You don't always get what I'm doing, but you DO always let me be me, and for that I'm truly grateful. Thanks to my co-authors Jina and Tim for their hard work on this book, and the SitePoint crew for getting me involved. Finally, huge thanks go to my co-workers Jeff Smith and Joanna Briggs for all their support and assistance with this and everything we do. I'm proud that you're part of the team. Finally, thanks to Carolyn Wood who, in addition to being my friend, inspires me to be a better writer.

Chapter 1

Planning

Forms—maybe you love them, maybe you think they're … well … boring. Either way, forms are an essential part of web design and development. From small login forms to detailed administration panels, forms are one of the most important interactive elements of your web site or application. They're the carriers of data and—if you'll pardon the courier's cliché—should be handled with care.

The way you develop your forms can greatly impact various concerns:

- Usability—are your forms easy to understand and simple to use?
- Accessibility—are your forms available to people who are accessing your site in a non-traditional manner?
- Error prevention—do your forms help ensure that the information you're collecting is free of problems?

Creating good forms can be a complicated process for both designers and developers. There are a lot of factors that go into creating a form—planning, designing, structuring (with markup), styling (with CSS), and enhancing (with JavaScript)—it's a lot of work! But this work is worth it in the end: an error-free, accessible, and user-friendly form is a happy form, leading to happy users.

Throughout this book, we'll be guiding you through a start-to-finish workflow. We'll start with devising our forms, move on to working through markup and styling, and then laying on some JavaScript to enhance and support your forms.

The Elements of Forms

It's important to understand the various elements that make up a form, so that you're aware of what's available to you. Let's first look at some of the basic default elements. Then, we'll take a look at some examples of more advanced features that are possible through progressive enhancement with JavaScript.

Basic Elements

HTML provides for a number of form elements, each designed to accept various types of content. Whether it's booking a flight or ordering groceries online, chances are you can create a functional form with just these basic elements.

Text Fields

Text fields, like the fields in Figure 1.1, allow the user to type in whatever they like. It's possible to specify a maximum length, otherwise any text can be entered.

Figure 1.1. Input fields used for names

Radio Buttons

Sometimes, you need to limit the user's input to a set of predetermined values. **Radio buttons** provide an ideal solution if one choice only must be made by the user. These are often presented as small round buttons beside each option, as seen in Figure 1.2.

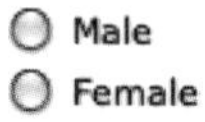

Figure 1.2. Radio buttons based on gender

Checkboxes

Checkboxes are another format for predetermined values, but allow for multiple values to be selected. You could use checkboxes to allow a person to choose several items. In Figure 1.3, we can see a series of checkboxes allowing a user to specify which vehicles they own. Most

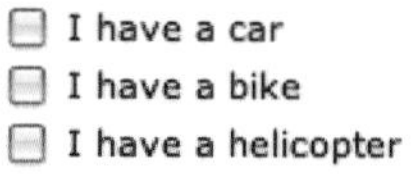

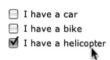

Figure 1.3. Multiple choices with checkboxes

browsers present checkboxes as squares; selected checkboxes have a tick or cross inside.

Labels

Labels are essential elements that tell you what the field represents. Most browsers make the space occupied by the label a clickable area, which helps increase the usability of the form; so rather than having to focus on a single, tiny button, a user can aim for the general area of its name. In Figure 1.4, we're clicking the checkboxes we saw in Figure 1.3; clicking the name will select the box.

☐ I have a car
☐ I have a bike
☑ I have a helicopter

Figure 1.4. Labels are clickable too!

Textareas

Hi Jina,

Thanks for the photos from the party! I can't believe how crazy my hair was!

Figure 1.5. A textarea as shown in Safari, with resizing handle

Textareas permit the user to type text, just like input fields, but they allow multiple lines of text to be entered. They can even scroll to accommodate content that exceeds the given width and height. In some browsers, such as Apple's Safari, these can even be resized by the user.

Select Menus

Select menus are yet another way to display predetermined values; this time, they're arranged as a menu. The benefit to using these over radio buttons or checkboxes is that they save on space, particularly if you have an extensive list of options. However, they're a little harder to use in terms of ergonomics (in that the user needs to hold down the button and drag simultaneously). If you only have a couple of choices, it might be best to just use radio buttons or checkboxes.

Figure 1.6. A drop-down select menu, closed (left) and open (center), and a select list (right)

Select menus come in two forms: **drop-downs** and **select lists**. Drop-downs, as shown in Figure 1.6, are employed when the user may select only one of the choices. Select lists, like the one to the right of Figure 1.6, are used when the reader can make multiple selections.

The options contained within a select menu may also be grouped, as shown in Figure 1.7.

Figure 1.7. Option groups

File Upload

File upload fields are used for … well, uploading files. Perhaps you're uploading some photos to your favorite social network, adding a PDF attachment to an online job application, or sharing a snippet of code on a forum. Pressing the button to

Figure 1.8. The file upload field on a Mac

select a file will open your operating system's file chooser; from here, you pick the file you want to use.

Fieldsets and Legends

Fieldsets and **legends** are very helpful for organizing forms, especially if they're lengthy forms. They're a way to group related fields together, which can enhance accessibility and usability. The fieldset is the element that contains the group; below, in Figure 1.9, it's represented by the gray line around the fields. The legend is the text shown at the top of that fieldset: **Personalia**.

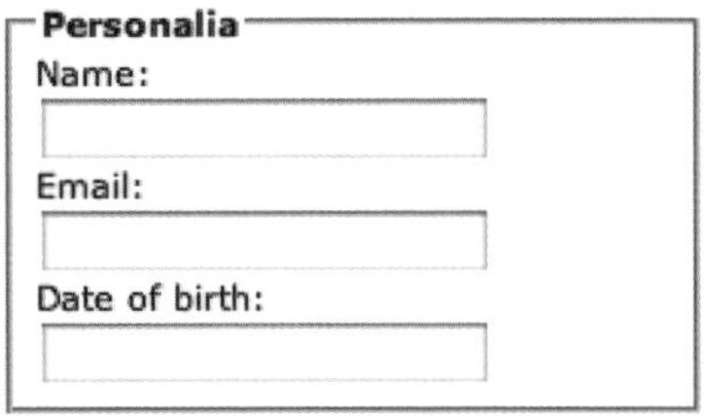

Figure 1.9. Fields contained within a fieldset

Buttons

Last, but certainly not least, we'll need a button to submit the form, like the one in Figure 1.10. Most browsers present these in a manner that suggests they're clickable—a raised or rounded effect, or sometimes both, as shown in Figure 1.10.

Figure 1.10. Click Me!

Enhanced Elements

While the basic form elements we just covered can handle most kinds of forms, progressive enhancements (typically implemented with JavaScript) can help make certain tasks easier, clearer, or more efficient. The best fancy form elements are **unobtrusive**, meaning that there's a way to use the form when JavaScript is unavailable in the browser. Let's look at some examples of enhanced form elements.

Split Buttons with Menus

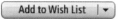

Figure 1.11. Amazon's Wish List button, above, with menu, below

Split buttons are becoming increasingly popular. The button itself will perform a certain action, such as adding an item to a cart; however, a part of the button—often indicated by a segregated area on the right with a downward arrow—will trigger a drop-down menu with other options relating to that action. An example of this can be found with Amazon's[1] Add to Wish List buttons, shown in Figure 1.11. Clicking the main part of the button will add an item to your Wish List, while clicking the arrow at the right edge will reveal a box with further options.

Sliders

Sliders can be used to indicate a number or range. These normally take the form of one control that moves across a bar to indicate the desired amount or value, or with two controls indicating minimum and maximum values, such as time or quantity.

Figure 1.12. Time ranges for flights on Kayak

My favorite use for a range slider is at Kayak,[2] where a slider is used to help you choose acceptable flight times when booking a flight. As you can see in Figure 1.12, this widget uses two handles on the slider's range bar so that you can indicate a start and end time for your flight's departure and return.

Toggle Switches

A **toggle switch** can be used for two either/or choices: for example, on/off, true/false, or public/private. Brightkite,[3] a location-based social network, uses this feature to allow members to quickly switch profiles from public to private and vice versa; this is handy for situations in which you want to quickly and temporarily make your profile public (like when you're attending a conference). In Figure 1.13, you'll see Brightkite's toggle in action.

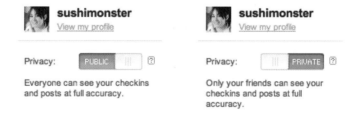

Figure 1.13. Now you see me, now you don't

---

[2] http://kayak.com/
[3] http://brightkite.com/

Auto-completion

Auto-completion is an ideal way to help the user complete fields quicker; it also helps avoid multiple spellings or variations of one specific entry. An example of this can be found in Facebook's profile editor,[4] when filling out your hometown. As you type, a menu appears below the text box displaying a list of possible matches for the city or town you've begun typing. This helps avoid misspellings on the city name or the wrong selection. For example, as seen in Figure 1.14, there are a number of towns named Nashville, so it's important to ensure that you select the right one.

Figure 1.14. Which Nashville?

---

[4] http://facebook.com/

Date Pickers

Date pickers make choosing a date easier, especially when it might be far off into the future. The ability to see exactly which day of the week a certain date will fall on helps when booking trips or making appointments. Date pickers normally take the form of a calendar. In Figure 1.15, a screenshot from Dopplr,[5] we can see an example of a calendar-style date picker being used for an upcoming trip.

Figure 1.15. Selecting an upcoming date on Dopplr

Color Pickers

Color pickers are usually found in web applications that allow you to customize your site experience or your profile. Some users are unfamiliar with hexadecimal color code—the system used in web development to specify color—or they may lack the tools to help them find that information. Color pickers enable these users to select the color they want, though a good color picker still provides the ability to enter a hex code.

Figure 1.16 shows Virb's[6] color picker in action.

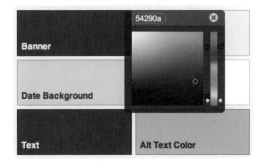

Figure 1.16. Virb's color picker, with hex code entry field at the top of the window

---

[5] http://dopplr.com/
[6] http://virb.com/

Advanced File Uploaders

An **advanced file uploader** can help make uploading multiple files faster and easier. This feature is often found on social networking sites that have photo albums. Flickr's file uploader—shown in Figure 1.17—permits multiple uploads, shows the upload progress of each file, and indicates the size of the files.

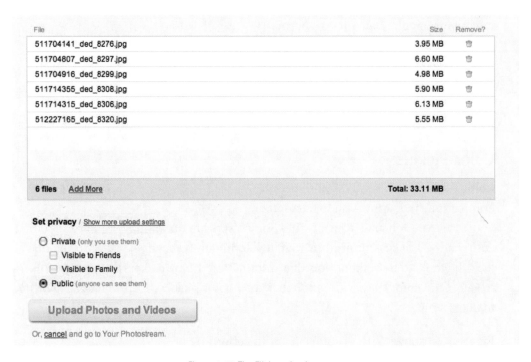

Figure 1.17. The Flickr uploader

Rich Text Editors

Rich text editors enhance the good old textarea by allowing content to be formatted and styled easily. This is commonly found on blogging and content management web sites. In WordPress, the text entry field—shown in Figure 1.18—allows a user to construct a blog post in a familiar, intuitive editor. To the right, there's an HTML tab, so that HTML-savvy users can switch to this mode to view or edit the markup.

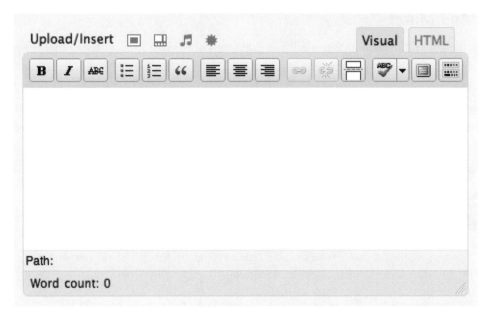

Figure 1.18. WordPress's rich text editor

Drag and Drop

Draggable items provide an intuitive way to reorder objects in a list or move items in and out of a target area. In Panic's T-shirt store,[7] seen in Figure 1.19, customers can pick up T-shirts and drop them into the cart area at the bottom of the screen.

Figure 1.19. Panic's shopping cart

---

[7] http://panic.com/goods/

... And More!

As designers and developers explore what's possible with form enhancement, new methods and techniques appear. As you use the Web, keep an eye out for unusual or innovative uses of form elements. When you spot a form that impresses you, it can be useful to take notes or a screenshot; savvy designers and developers keep a collection of interesting and innovative stuff for later reference. To start your own file, use a scrapbooking-style application like Evernote,[8] a service like Flickr,[9] or even just a collection of screenshots in a folder on your hard drive.

 Interaction Patterns

Jargon time! An **interaction pattern** is a way to describe a particular widget, function, or interactive element, describing the particular problems they solve and the rationale for using a given pattern.

Some keen collectors of interaction patterns make their collections available on the Web. At Welie.com,[10] you'll find dozens of different types of menus, widgets, and other interactive elements. The Yahoo Developer Network's Design Pattern Library[11] contains many patterns shown as videos, which makes it easy to understand how the interaction occurs. UI-Patterns[12] is a newer site with a small, but growing, collection. UI Pattern Factory[13] is based on a similar idea, with a growing collection of screenshots pulled from Flickr.

Research and Finding Inspiration

Before you dive into building your form, it's important to do your homework first. Forms are powerful, but without proper planning and design, they can make tasks overbearing or difficult. It's also good to look around for inspiration, for both the interaction and visual aspects of form design.

---

[8] http://evernote.com/
[9] http://flickr.com/
[10] http://welie.com/
[11] http://developer.yahoo.com/ypatterns/
[12] http://ui-patterns.com/
[13] http://uipatternfactory.com/

For this book, we'll be building a fictional social networking site, **Fit and Awesome**, for people that are into health and fitness. Members of the Fit and Awesome community will be able to store their statistics and training journals on the site, and share their fitness goals and activities with other members. Naturally, a site like this will require a number of different forms and widgets—there's plenty to sink our teeth into here!

Perform a Competitive Audit

Take a look at what web sites and applications similar to yours are doing. It's an ideal way to understand what's successful in other sites or to work out what fails to perform. If you're designing a social network, check out other social networks. How do different companies handle editing a profile? Or privacy settings? If you're working on an ecommerce web site, take a look at some of the successful competitors. Is their checkout process quick and easy, or is it tedious? Do you find yourself entering the same information over and over again?

As you're looking at competitors, take note of issues you come across as you try to use their product, as well as what works well. This information will be helpful in your brainstorming process. Look for possible areas of innovation while still considering established conventions; examine the reasons *why* a technique is effective or not.

In Figure 1.20, I've collected the registration forms for four different sites—Gimme20,[14] Fitness Magazine,[15] Fitness.com,[16] and SELF Magazine.[17] Each form has different features, questions, and interface elements, all of which are useful to consider.

---

[14] http://gimme20.com/
[15] http://fitnessmagazine.com/
[16] http://fitness.com/
[17] http://self.com/

Figure 1.20. The registration screens for Gimme20, SELF, Fitness.com, and Fitness Magazine

Use Software as Inspiration

Desktop software can be a worthwhile place to look for inspiration. These days, more and more web applications are beginning to look and feel like software. This can be good or bad—a poorly chosen desktop widget could confuse a user, and there are some interactions that just work better on the desktop than in a browser. When you're thinking about including a desktop-like widget in your site, try to be sure that you've chosen it because it's the right tool for the job, rather than because it's fashionable in desktop applications. Consider whether it's necessary. If you could do without it, chances are that you should leave it out.

Figure 1.21 shows the view size menu in Microsoft Word for the Mac; in many ways it resembles a regular select menu, which is hardly notable, but the range of choices and the order in which they're arranged could be a useful technique to emulate or improve upon.

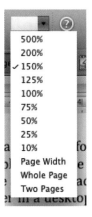

Shown below, in Figure 1.22, Coda's new site panel uses a series of collapsible sections to help a user make more sense of the various requirements. The form itself occupies only a small amount of space, and makes use of a scroll bar at the right. These are both suitable ways to help make sense of a larger form.

Figure 1.21. Microsoft Word's view size menu

Figure 1.22. Coda's new site panel, with collapsible sections

Interaction Design

Interaction design is the process of defining your interface's behavior. For form design, I can't stress enough how important it is. Having a solid, user-centered plan for your forms' designs is the best way to ensure that they're a success. This is where the design helps support a relationship between the form and the user.

Defining the Goal

An important part of planning any project is to define what's required. Writing up documentation, defining task flows, and performing testing may seem a dull, unexciting venture. However, some attention to detail can greatly improve and inform your design process; with a solid idea of what your forms ought to achieve, it's easier to create the solution that best fits the needs of your users. Fancy effects and graphics can make a form look and feel beautiful, but if it fails to provide the solution needed, then the design falls flat.

Creating documentation to describe the expected behavior of a system is an important task, and the resulting material is quite handy when you're working with others or for a client. This type of document is formally known as a **functional specification**.

Identify the Users

Who's going to be using these forms? Are the users tech savvy? Will they benefit from the fancy, progressive enhancements you're thinking about employing or will that actually be a hindrance for them? Some designers go as far as to create **user personas**, fictitious characters that help a designer define the needs and abilities of the kinds of people who'll use the site.[18] For my part, I prefer talking to real people that fit into the target audience. The following table contains a mini profile of four real people whose interests and abilities we'll use as a benchmark when we plan and build our forms.

---

[18] For a discussion of user personas and how to create your own, visit
http://www.hhs.gov/usability/analyze/personas.html

Persona	Profile
Derek Featherstone	Fitness Interests: Triathlons, cycle trainers Technical Level: Very comfortable with the Web
Jina Bolton	Fitness Interests: Gym, casual cycling, WiiFit Technical Level: Very comfortable with the Web
Kelly Steele	Fitness Interests: Casual cycling, tennis, gym Technical Level: Moderately comfortable with the Web
Mathew Walker	Fitness Interests: Basketball, golf Technical Level: New to the Web

Identify Use Cases and Scenarios

While considering the people that will be using your forms, you should think about the various **use cases** that go along with them: so as well as defining the people who'll use your site and their goals, this is about how they can reach those goals using the forms on your site.

Use cases help you answer a number of important questions. What do you (or your client) require? How will the form's data be used? For registering an account on a social network, will members be required to fill the form out in its entirety, or can they just fill out the basics and complete it at a later time? What information should remain public? Should certain kinds of information be kept private? Why would someone register in the first place, and what's important to them?

Understand Platforms and Devices

You might be using the latest version of Safari on your nice big MacBook Air, but another user filling out the form could be an everyday commuter browsing on their Blackberry.

When you're planning a form, it's important to consider all the platforms and devices that may be used for your forms, or you might cause a lot of heartache! For instance, I use Yelp[19] for looking up restaurants, and occasionally I submit reviews. I would love to write these reviews as soon as I've left the restaurant, but I never do. Why? Because the form is horribly annoying and tedious to use on my iPhone.

Below, we've specified a number of browsers which we'll use to test and refine our form design.

Desktop   Safari 3, Firefox 2, Internet Explorer 6+ (limited functionality)

Mobile   Generic mobile CSS, iPhone-specific

Define Task Flows

Now that you've given some careful consideration to the users, use cases, and platforms, you should now have enough information to plot out the steps needed to complete each form—**a task flow**. It's also time to think about alternate paths and error cases. Sketch it out visually, so that you have a clear idea of what your process looks like; Figure 1.23 shows us an example of a task flow diagram for a sign-up and login form.

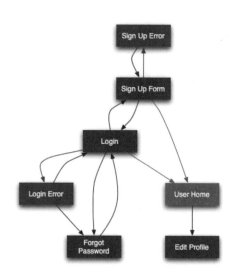

Figure 1.23. A task flow example for signing up or logging in

---

[19] http://yelp.com/

By this stage you should have a fairly solid idea of what's required in your form. It's now time to put pen to paper!

Paper Prototyping

Creating a **paper prototype** of your form is a quick and easy way to hash out your ideas and issues at the beginning of the form development process. Draw your forms on paper: keep it fast, lightweight, and simple, sketching out a basic idea of how each form would look. You can even use a quick and cheap option like a stack of sticky notes; if you use a note for each object in your form, it's easy to experiment with different arrangements. Use this hand-drawn form to assess how your form looks so far. It's amazing how much more clearer your decisions about form questions become when you see them in front of you.

Try the prototype out on your peers—they might see stuff you missed. If it's okay to show your forms to the public at this stage, perhaps you could head over to the closest café and try them out on some complete strangers after buying them a cup of coffee.

For a great, detailed introduction to paper prototyping, check out Shawn Medero's article in A List Apart.[20]

Wireframing

Now that you've completed your planning, it's time to start designing. Begin with rough diagrams or **wireframes** before obsessing over the shiny buttons. What we're focusing on right now is the layout. The diagrams you'll see over the next few pages, from Figure 1.24 to Figure 1.29, are wireframes for our example site.

Notice that they're plain, clean, and simple—there's no need for a lot of detail or intricate design work here. Right now, we're only hashing out the basic flow and general layout.

---

[20] http://alistapart.com/articles/paperprototyping

Sign Up

Already a member? Log in.

Hi there! We're excited to have you as a part of our community. To get started, please create an account.

Your email address

Create password

Confirm password

Your profile link   fitandawesome.com/

Birth date   Month ⌃⌄   Day ⌃⌄   Year ⌃⌄

This is hidden by default from your profile.

☐   I have read and agree to the T.O.S.

create profile >

Figure 1.24. Sign Up wireframe

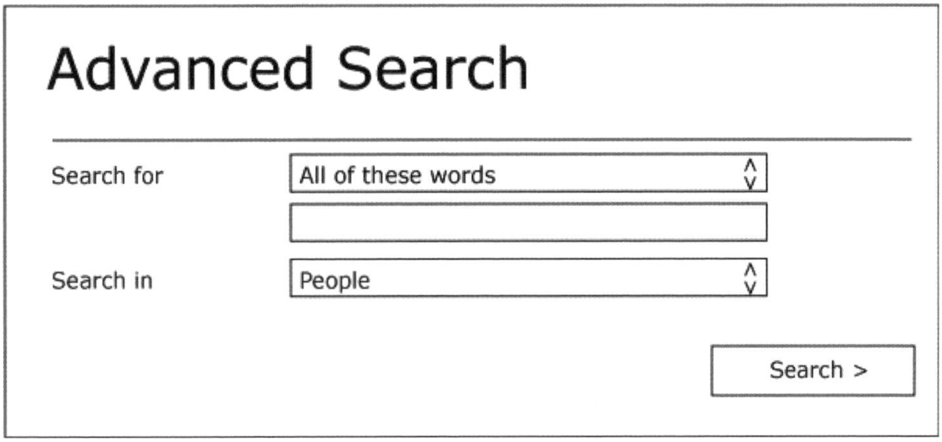

Advanced Search

Search for | All of these words | ∧∨ |

[   ]

Search in | People | ∧∨ |

[Search >]

Figure 1.25. Advanced Search wireframe

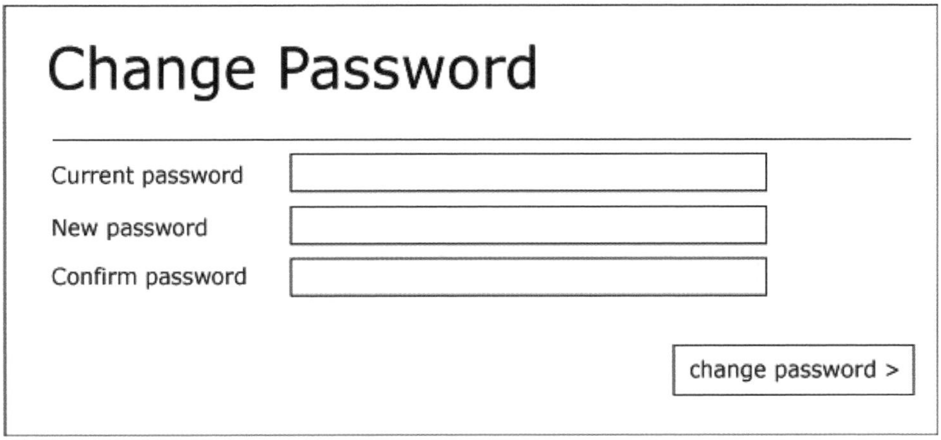

Change Password

Current password   [   ]

New password   [   ]

Confirm password   [   ]

[change password >]

Figure 1.26. Change Password wireframe

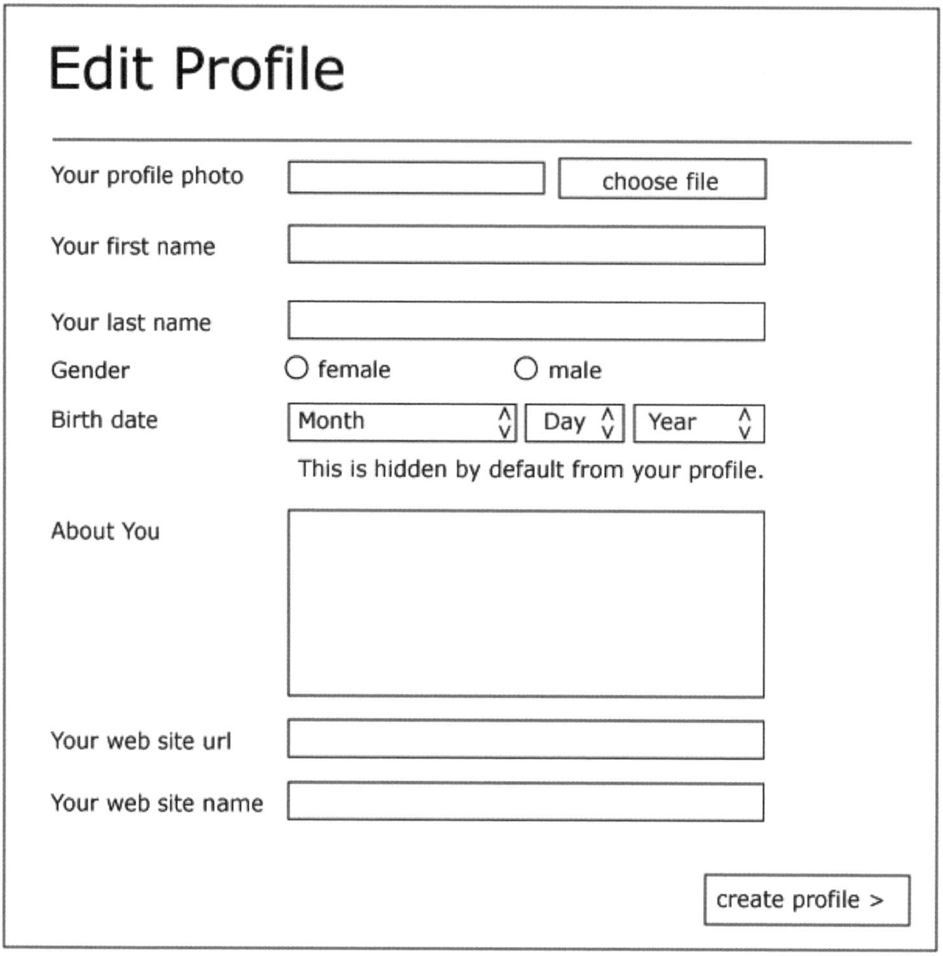

Edit Profile

Your profile photo [ ] [choose file]

Your first name [ ]

Your last name [ ]

Gender   ○ female   ○ male

Birth date   [Month ˄˅] [Day ˄˅] [Year ˄˅]

This is hidden by default from your profile.

About You [ ]

Your web site url [ ]

Your web site name [ ]

[create profile >]

Figure 1.27. Edit Profile wireframe

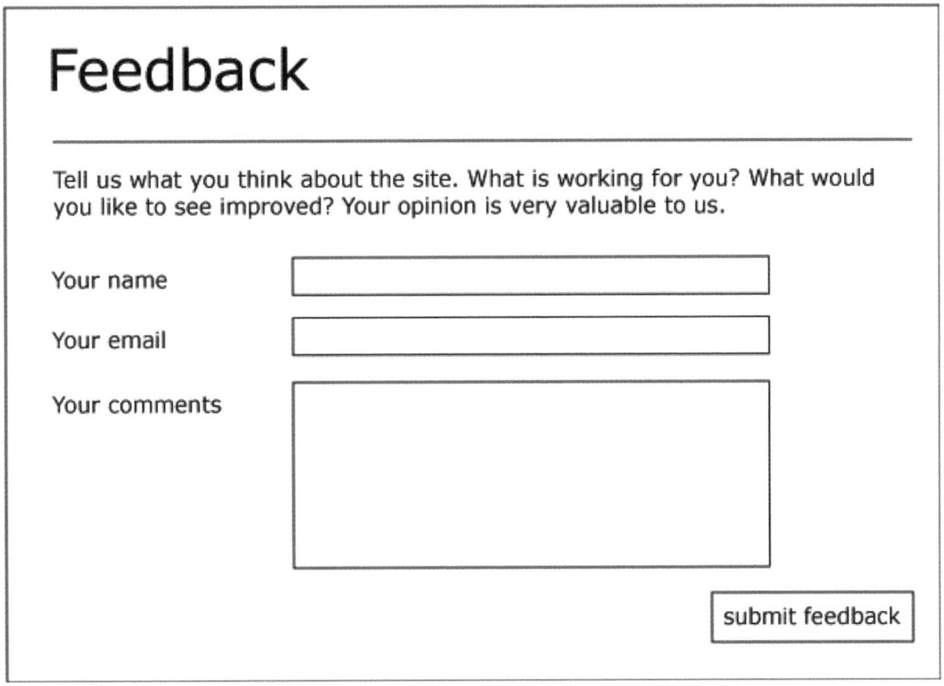

Feedback

Tell us what you think about the site. What is working for you? What would you like to see improved? Your opinion is very valuable to us.

Your name

Your email

Your comments

submit feedback

Figure 1.28. Feedback wireframe

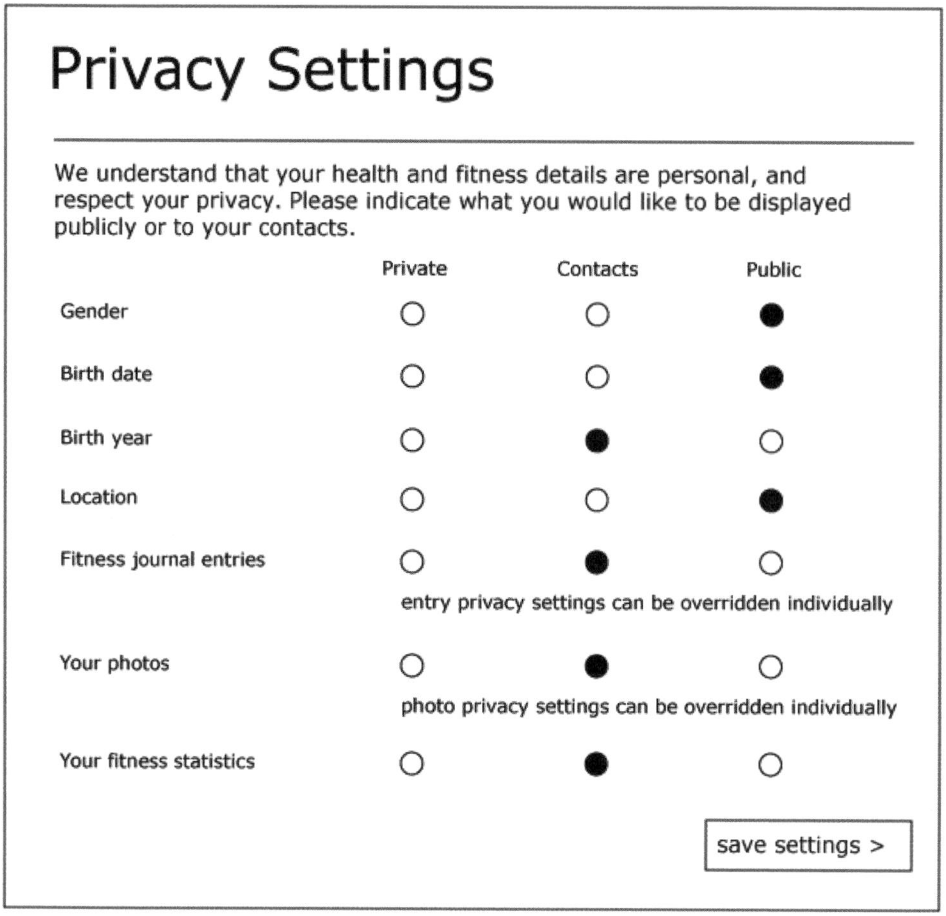

Privacy Settings

We understand that your health and fitness details are personal, and respect your privacy. Please indicate what you would like to be displayed publicly or to your contacts.

	Private	Contacts	Public
Gender	○	○	●
Birth date	○	○	●
Birth year	○	●	○
Location	○	○	●
Fitness journal entries	○	●	○

entry privacy settings can be overridden individually

Your photos	○	●	○

photo privacy settings can be overridden individually

Your fitness statistics	○	●	○

save settings >

Figure 1.29. Privacy Settings wireframe

Summary

In this chapter we've explored the many elements of forms and why it's vital to develop your forms with an eye to usability, accessibility, and error-free data. We've looked at some of the basic elements like radio buttons, form fields, and select menus, and explored some of the enhanced features available like sliders and color pickers. We've covered the importance of research; talked about methods for drawing inspiration for your form creation; and looked at the process of interaction design, which involves specifications, prototypes, and wireframes.

Believe it or not, you're already halfway there to your goal of creating seriously fancy forms! You might be wondering how that's possible, as you've barely started this book. Well, proper planning is *that* important, and will save you a lot of headaches later. Trust me on this!

Now that we have a firm idea of the general contents and layout of the form, it's time to design the interface.

Designing

In Chapter 1, we focused on the planning phase of fancy form design. With the interaction nailed down, we've actually begun the design process for the forms. Now, we're going to look at the visual design side of form design.

Visual design can either enhance or detract from usability, depending on its implementation. It's important to know how to use visual design in a way that enhances the form's usability, as well as making it aesthetically pleasing. In this chapter, we'll take a look at:

- grid and typography
- color
- imagery

Grid and Typography

When we created the wireframes for the form, we'd already begun the process of thinking about our form's layout. Now, we can tighten the grid and think about proportions and layout patterns, creating a structure for the visual design of our form. Then, we can tune our typography so that our form is legible and clear.

Grid Systems

The **grid** is one of the most fundamental elements of graphic design. It provides a solid foundation for placement of elements within the design of our forms. Using consistent grid systems throughout your web site or application is good for brand stewardship and usability, as well as organization.[1]

For Fit and Awesome, we'll use Figure 2.1 for our forms.

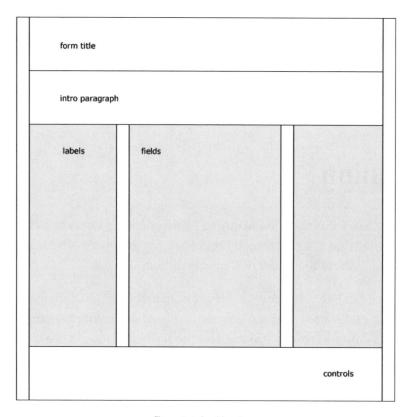

Figure 2.1. A grid system

---

[1] Some company brands have guidelines that go beyond fonts, colors, and logos; grid patterns are an ideal way to have a united and organized look and feel across materials, whether it's pages in a brochure, billboard ads, or in our case, forms used on a web site.

- The top section is the form's header, which will display the form's title.
- Directly beneath the header is room for an introductory paragraph, if required.
- Then, the form is broken into three columns:
  1. The first column is where we'll place our main labels for our form elements.
  2. The second column is where we'll place those form elements (`inputs`, `textareas`, `select` menus, and so on).
  3. The third column is blank for now, but can be used for messages or other contextual elements, like icons.
- Below the columns is an area for controls or buttons.

Of course, like any system there'll almost certainly be exceptions to the rule: it's okay to break out of the grid from time to time, as the design and interactivity of a form can change based on your goals and those of your users. We've kept our grid system quite simple to allow plenty of flexibility.

Type

A form that's easy to read is likely to be a form that's easy to use. This is especially important for forms that have multiple sections or steps, so that users avoid feeling overwhelmed or lost. Figure 2.2 shows our Sign Up form with elements placed within a grid system—but with poor typography, it's difficult to read. Since every bit of text looks more or less the same, it's harder to scan through the text.

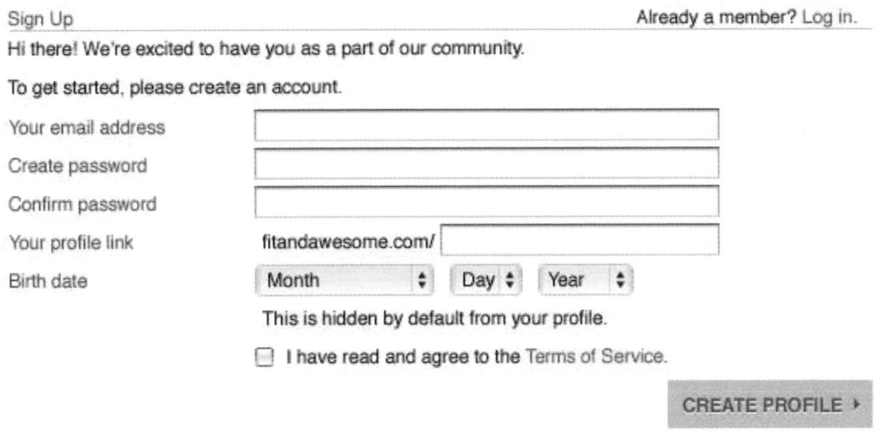

Figure 2.2. Poor typography makes this form difficult for the eye

Let's improve on it. In Figure 2.3, we've added various weights, sizes, and shades to our text to provide contrast and a hierarchy. There's also more space around each form question. With these simple adjustments, the form already feels a little more organized and is easier to read.

Sign Up

Already a member? Log in.

Hi there! We're excited to have you as a part of our community.
To get started, please create an account.

Your email address

Create password

Confirm password

Your profile link   fitandawesome.com/

Birth date   Month ⬍   Day ⬍   Year ⬍

This is hidden by default from your profile.

☐ I have read and agree to the Terms of Service.

Figure 2.3. Much better!

Naturally, we can improve this further with some additional color.

Color

Color is, of course, a great way to make our forms look more interesting, but there's more to it than that. While grid systems help us organize the placement of elements, color systems can help emphasize an item's importance or meaning, making for a much more usable interaction. An example would be using color to indicate an error state, or to highlight a required field.

Highlighting Calls to Action

A **call to action** is a phrase used in interaction design that refers to the action you'd like your user to take. In the case of a form, the call to action often concerns the user entering some details or clicking a button in order to complete a particular task.

Primary calls to action associated with a form may include an Add to Cart button, a Sign In button, or a Post Entry button. It's a good idea to use noticeable, bold colors for these types of buttons. Secondary calls, such as a Cancel button, can use subtler, muted tones, to show that they're of less importance.

In Figure 2.4, we see an example of this used at West Elm,[2] an ecommerce site that sells furniture and home décor. The primary call to action here is to encourage users to add a product to the shopping bag, so the **Add to Shopping Bag** button uses a darker gray. It stands out more than **Add to My Project**, which uses a lighter shade.

Figure 2.4. West Elm's calls to action

While shades of gray are capable of doing the trick, we'd like to use some green for the primary call to action in our forms for two reasons: the color will make the button more obvious, and it will complement the overall color scheme of the rest of our site.

Figure 2.5. Preview and Save buttons

In our Edit Profile form, saving the form is our primary call to action, so we've used green to ensure that it stands out more than the light gray-shaded preview button.

The Message of Color

When choosing colors, be aware of the message that each color may convey. Greens connote a positive tone—they send the message that it's okay to proceed, or that an action you performed was successful. Reds can signal a negative outcome: highlighting an error, or advising that your action may cause an undesired effect, such as canceling an activity or deleting a profile.

While color helps add hierarchy and meaning, it's important to remember that color is just one of many methods for indicating a message. Some users are unable to see color; they may be color-blind or visually-impaired, or they may use a device that only displays in grayscale, such as Amazon's Kindle ebook reader. Use a mix of icons, color, or text to indicate the fields that need attention. Some forms will explain the errors and omissions at the top of the form as text, as well as beside the fields.

In Figure 2.6, red is an appropriate color to indicate fields that were filled out incorrectly. Yet, there's also a message above the form which explains the problem, so that the meaning of the problem is clear regardless of whether the user comprehends the color red, or not.

Figure 2.6. A message explains the problem, while a border highlights the incorrect field

Imagery

Imagery can add a nice touch to your forms, enhancing the design. More importantly, imagery can be used to provide additional context, such as highlighting an error or a required field in the form.

Iconography

Icons can be a highly effective visual indicator. Let's think again of our error message shown above, in Figure 2.6; this is an ideal place for an icon, and helps to further emphasize the error field. We'll place the icon to the right, which you can see below in Figure 2.7:

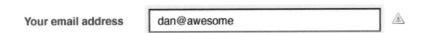

Figure 2.7. Adding an icon to the error message

Background Patterns and Textures

Subtle background patterns and textures help add volume and depth to a form. While it may seem a purely aesthetic consideration, textures that add dimension to a form can go a long way to improving its usability. Rather than being merely a bunch of flat rectangles, these form elements seem to lift from the page—they feel more authentic because their interactive nature is emphasized.

Here's our Sign Up form so far, in Figure 2.8. Our typography changes have helped lift the text, and the color on the Create Profile button is an improvement, but overall this is hardly a fancy form!

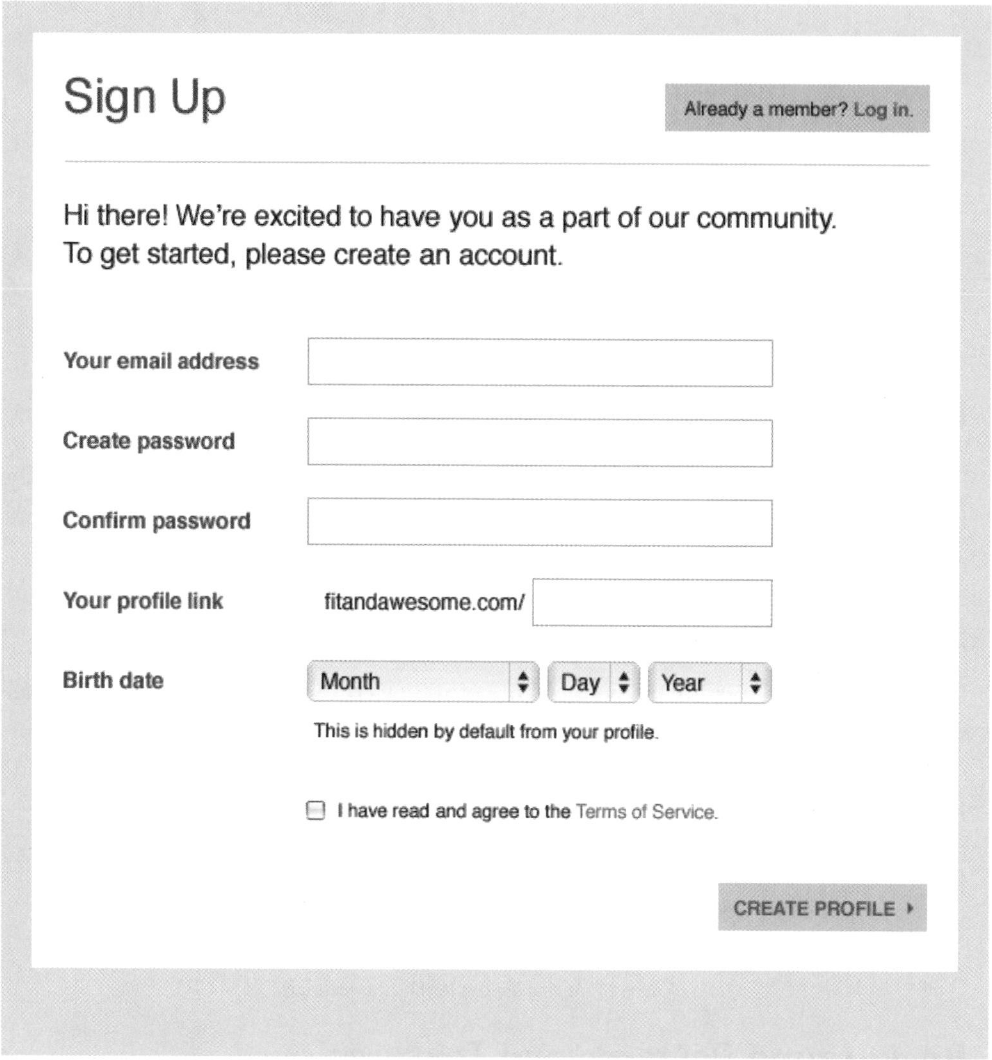

Sign Up

Already a member? Log in.

Hi there! We're excited to have you as a part of our community. To get started, please create an account.

Your email address

Create password

Confirm password

Your profile link   fitandawesome.com/

Birth date   Month ⏶⏷ Day ⏶⏷ Year ⏶⏷

This is hidden by default from your profile.

☐ I have read and agree to the Terms of Service.

CREATE PROFILE ›

Figure 2.8. Our simple form is still a little drab

Now, let's add some depth and texture to the form. As seen in Figure 2.9, gradients and shadows provide definition: the fields are set off with a light gray background, making each field more distinctive. It's also a useful way to associate text with relevant sections, as seen under the birth date fields. Adding a raised effect to the Create Profile button helps to emphasize this important element, too. Overall, it's a much friendlier, more usable form!

Sign Up

Already a member? Log in.

Hi there! We're excited to have you as a part of our community. To get started, please create an account.

Your email address

Create password

Confirm password

Your profile link   fitandawesome.com/

Birth date   Month ⬍   Day ⬍   Year ⬍
                     This is hidden by default from your profile.

☐ I have read and agree to the Terms of Service.

CREATE PROFILE ▸

Figure 2.9. Gradients, shadows, and texture help this form pop!

Let's take a look at the rest of our forms with the new grid, typography, color, and image styles applied, seen in Figure 2.10 through to Figure 2.14.

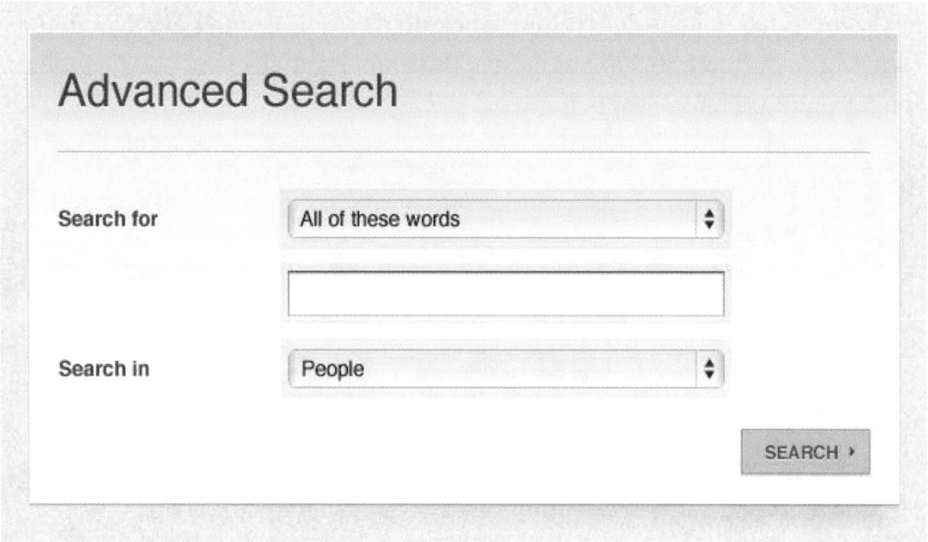

Figure 2.10. Advanced Search

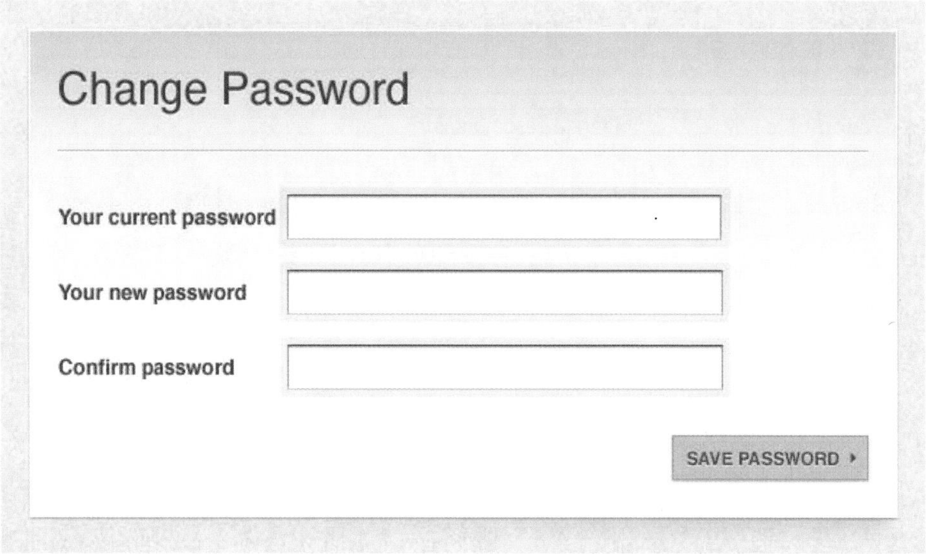

Figure 2.11. Change Password

Edit Profile

Your profile photo   [   ] [Browse]

Your first name   [   ]

Your last name   [   ]

Gender   ● Female   ○ Male

Birthday   [Month ▲▼] [Day ▲▼] [Year ▲▼]

This is hidden by default from your profile.

About You   [   ]

Your website address   [   ]

Website name   [   ]

[PREVIEW PROFILE] [SAVE ▸]

Figure 2.12. Edit Profile

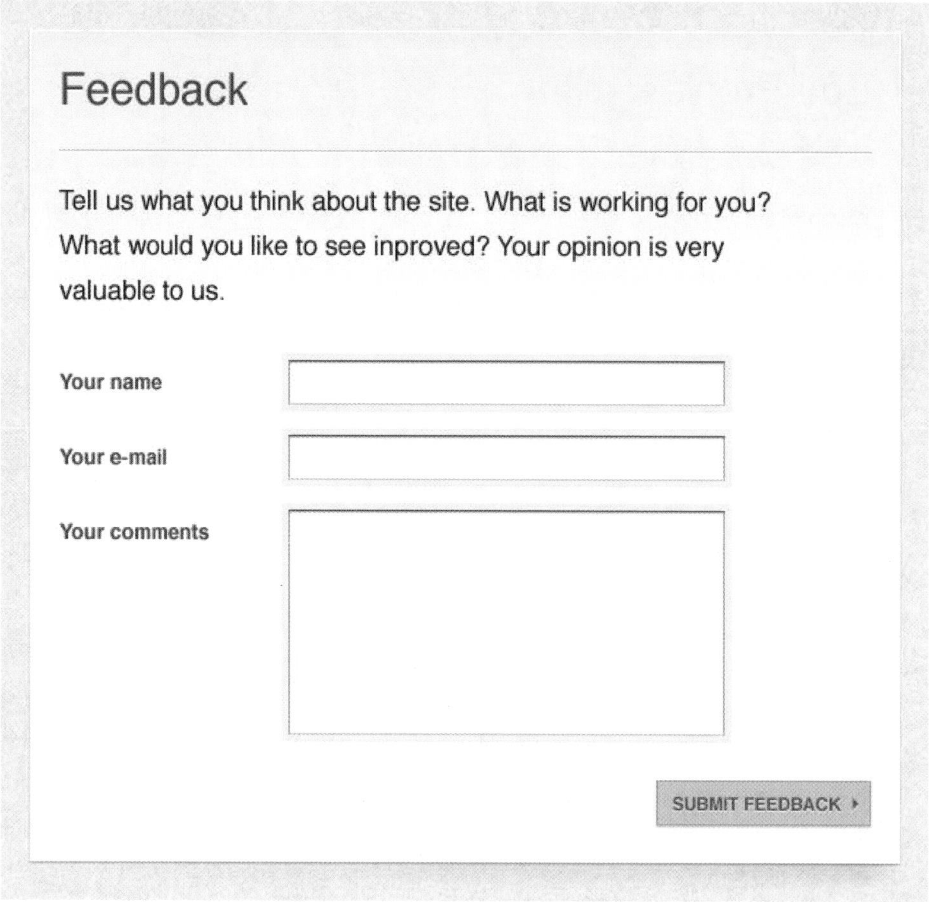

Feedback

Tell us what you think about the site. What is working for you? What would you like to see inproved? Your opinion is very valuable to us.

Your name

Your e-mail

Your comments

SUBMIT FEEDBACK ▸

Figure 2.13. Feedback

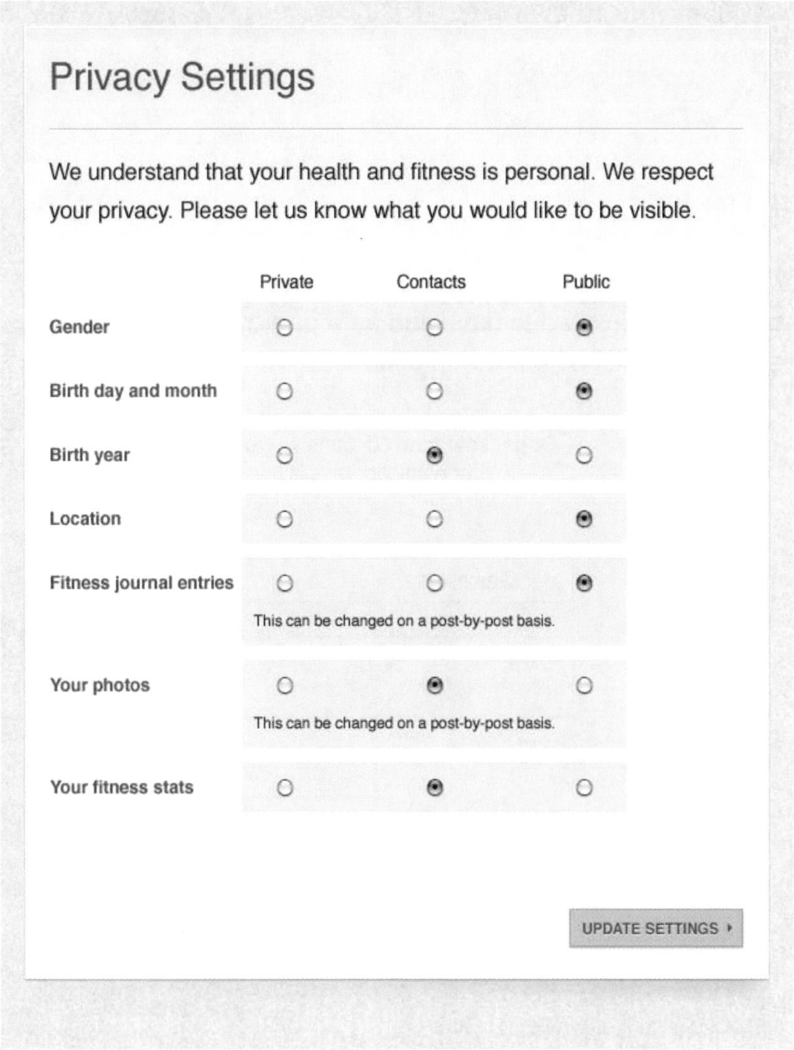

Privacy Settings

We understand that your health and fitness is personal. We respect your privacy. Please let us know what you would like to be visible.

	Private	Contacts	Public
Gender	○	○	◉
Birth day and month	○	○	◉
Birth year	○	◉	○
Location	○	○	◉
Fitness journal entries	○	○	◉

This can be changed on a post-by-post basis.

	Private	Contacts	Public
Your photos	○	◉	○

This can be changed on a post-by-post basis.

	Private	Contacts	Public
Your fitness stats	○	◉	○

UPDATE SETTINGS ›

Figure 2.14. Privacy Settings

Figure 2.15 shows a detail from our Sign Up form, this time showing the error state and informative message.

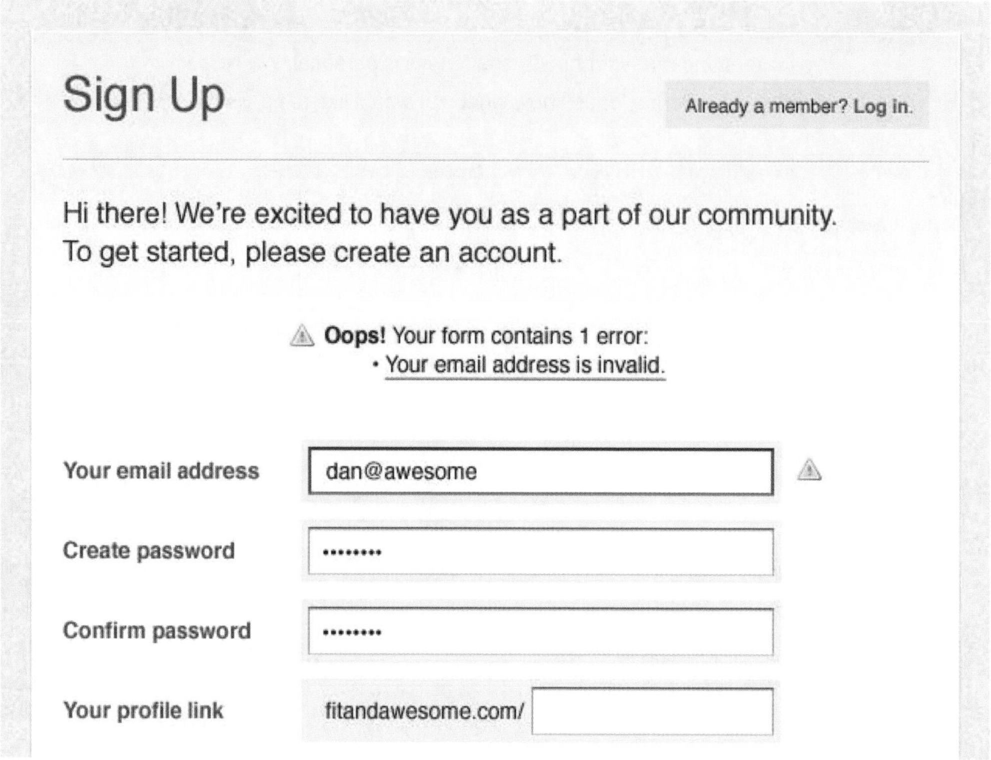

Sign Up

Already a member? Log in.

Hi there! We're excited to have you as a part of our community. To get started, please create an account.

⚠ **Oops!** Your form contains 1 error:
• Your email address is invalid.

Your email address	dan@awesome ⚠
Create password	••••••••
Confirm password	••••••••
Your profile link	fitandawesome.com/

Figure 2.15. Oops!

Summary

In this chapter we discussed the value of strong visual design: as well as adding to the aesthetic appeal of forms, it should also enhance the usability experience for users. We looked at how well-structured grid systems and clear typography are necessary for layout and legibility. We examined how color can be employed to great effect, especially when used to highlight a primary call to action, but also that it's important to be mindful of what different colors can signify. Alongside this, we established that color should always be used in conjunction with other indicators, as some users—for various reasons—are unable to view color. Finally, we looked at how imagery such as iconography or background patterns and textures can be implemented to create further volume and depth.

With elegant and creative use of typography, grid, color, and imagery, your forms should have a much fancier experience—planned out well, and designed to be hot stuff, too! We're now ready to move on to the next step: structuring the form with markup.

Chapter **3**

Structure

We now need to address how to organize forms. We've spent time in the last chapter looking at ways of visually organizing things so that they make sense and display visual hierarchy, rhythm, grouping, and consistency. And we created that grid for a reason, right? Establishing those visual characteristics for the way the forms are laid out makes it easier to understand—at least for those of us that can see it. What do we do, then, for those that may be blind, for example, or using an alternative device to access your site? How do we translate that into information that's meaningful for those unable to see our gorgeous, fancy form design? The answer is simple—we go right back to structure.

There is no set structure for forms; no formula that will fit all scenarios. A form that works well in a popular social networking site might be quite inappropriate for a company's payroll interface. Yet form consistency and predictability is one of the hallmarks for good interaction design.

How do we reconcile this? An approach such as the one we're using here in this book—a form grid with set widths and positions for each form field—is a useful tool in the real world as well. However, like any system, there'll always be exceptions to the rule: as the requirements of a form change along with the goals and needs of the user and the site owner, we often find we need to step outside the grid.

Let's take a look at the forms that we've been working with so far. In Chapter 2, we produced forms for each of the following tasks:

- Sign Up
- Advanced Search
- Password Utilities (a tool for forgotten passwords, and a tool to change your password)
- Edit Profile
- Feedback
- Privacy Settings

In addition to the forms themselves, we must pay careful attention to the variety of messages that we need to provide to users—advice and instructions, orientation information, and status messages that indicate error or success states. We need to ensure that we mark these up in a way that's accessible to all users—this can be easy to overlook if we forget to think about structure first. We have strong visuals for these forms, but when we're implementing that vision we need to think structure first, and that brings us right to the heart of the *lingua franca* of the Web: HTML.

The Structure of a Form

A lot depends on the HTML we use to construct our forms: it has to be flexible, providing enough structure for our CSS to hook into so that we can implement our design, yet sympathetic to accessibility issues. Surprisingly, navigating these issues only requires minimal, but careful, consideration.

Understanding the `form` Element

The foundation of any form is the `form` element. It wraps around the set of form fields that hold the data you wish to submit, and specifies two important points for the form element's attributes:

```
<form method="post" action="form-processor.php">
```

The `method` attribute contains one of two values, `post` or `get`. When sending a form using the `get` method, all of the data for the form is passed as part of the URL. When sent using the `post` method, the data is sent in the background, without being exposed at all in the URL. For this reason, `post` is generally the preferred method of sending form data. Meanwhile, the `action` attribute contains the URL for the back-end script that will process the form.

When `get` Has a Place

There is one instance where using the `get` method is better than using `post` and that's with search forms. The `get` method passes the search query parameters as part of the URL and enables the search form user to bookmark the results page and return at a later date. The user can also use the browser's back and forward buttons without the confusing "Resend form data?" browser warnings.

Form elements really are that simple! There are other attributes for the form element, though these are more rarely used. For a complete reference listing of attributes for the form element, see the SitePoint HTML Reference.[1] You can also read the World Wide Web Consortium's specification.[2]

While the `form` element is required, it's hardly the most exciting part of your form. Let's look at the elements that comprise the contents of your form.

Groups and Labels: `fieldset`, `legend`, and `label`

Basic form structure is provided by three elements that HTML provides: `fieldset`, `legend`, and `label`. These elements work together to group related fields. This paradigm comes from a long history of GUI design—long before the rise of the Web. If you look at almost any dialog box from any piece of software, you'll find the desktop application equivalent of a `fieldset` and `legend`.

---

[1] http://reference.sitepoint.com/html/form/
[2] http://www.w3.org/TR/html4/interact/forms.html#edef-FORM

In Figure 3.1, we can see an example of this concept from a Firefox preferences pane. Here you can see three sections on the active tab: **Accessibility**, **Browsing**, and **System Defaults**.

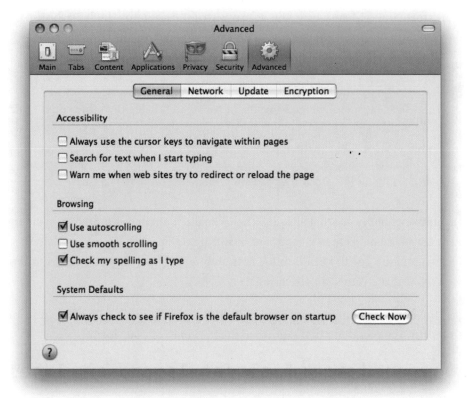

Figure 3.1. Tabs in the Firefox preferences dialog

If we were creating a similar layout in HTML, there would be three `fieldset` elements wrapped around each of the groups of checkboxes, as well as around the **Check Now** button. **Accessibility**, **Browsing**, and **System Defaults** would be the equivalent of the `legend` in HTML.

Fieldsets and legends are certainly optional, and in some cases might even be overkill for simple forms. In fact, most forms are unlikely to need them. However, they're a potentially useful tool for increasing the accessibility of our forms. Visually, we can see that each set of checkboxes in that dialog are separate groups, because of the way they're arranged. However, the use of that group heading—the `legend`, in HTML terms—provides additional context to say what each set of options is for. And that's precisely the context that `legend` provides in an HTML form.

Let's take a look at this in one of our forms, the **Change Password** form. It's shown below, unstyled, in Figure 3.2.

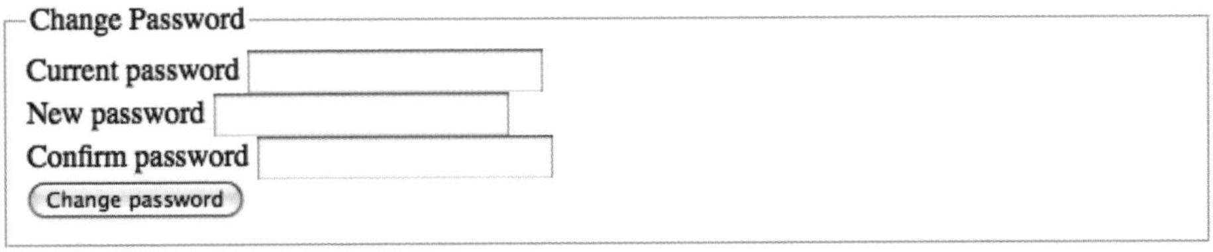

Figure 3.2. Our unstyled Change Password form

It might seem quite reasonable to say that the text **Change Password** should be enclosed in a `legend` element, found within a fieldset containing those fields. The markup for that might look a little like this:

```
<fieldset>
  <legend>Change Password</legend>

  : change password form fields

</fieldset>
```

This structure makes perfect sense, and we've heard many times before that `legends` and `fieldsets` are useful for accessibility. So this should be accessible, right? Oh, if only it were that simple. This is a case of how a well-intentioned tweak done for accessibility reasons may be unhelpful, and might even make it worse.

Here's why: a screen reader, such as JAWS, announces the `legend` text before each field label as the user tabs through the page. When a user working with JAWS interacts with this form, they'll hear the text of the `legend`, then the label, then the type of field.

How would that sound for this form? For the current password field they'd hear the screen reader say "Change Password, Your Current password, password." When they move to the new password field and the confirm password field they'll hear

"Change Password, Your New password, password" and "Change Password, Confirm password, password," respectively. It's as if we were playing a trick on the screen reader to see how many times can we prompt it to say "password." Technically accessible—it uses all the right elements—but a real pain to listen to.

The use of `fieldset` and `legend` is complicated further by the fact that screen readers differ across settings regarding whether they'll announce the text of the `legend` by default. JAWS, generally accepted as the most popular screen reader, does announce it by default, but Window-Eyes does not. For this simple form, the use of the `legend` element is likely to be overkill. There are enough cues in the labels of the form fields to give us enough context to understand what the fields are. Combine that with the point that password fields are announced by the screen reader, and there is more than enough information for a user to understand what they're supposed to do with that form.

We still need a title for the form, so rather than `legend`, we'll use an `h1` element. The change in our markup, shown in Figure 3.3, is simple:

```
<h1>Change Password</h1>
<fieldset>

  : change password form fields

</fieldset>
```

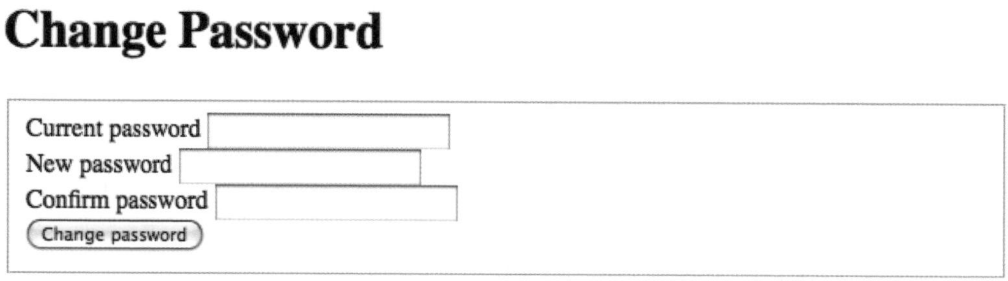

Change Password

Figure 3.3. The Change Password form without the legend

Let's use this knowledge to think about a different form: the **Sign Up** form we showed in the previous chapter. While we're wisely omitting the `legend` from the `fieldset` surrounding the form (can you imagine how annoying that would be?), adding `fieldset` and `legend` elements to sections within the form is worth exploring.

The birth date fields, shown unstyled in Figure 3.4, would indeed benefit from grouping. When we think about what it would sound like to a screen reader user, it becomes fairly clear that the extra information provided by using the `legend` is much less repetitive and annoying here than the legends on the **Change Password** form.

```
┌─Birth date──────────────────────────────────────────┐
│  Month  – Month – ♦                                   │
│  Day   – Day – ♦                                      │
│  Year   – Year – ♦                                    │
│  This is hidden by default from your profile.         │
└──────────────────────────────────────────────────────┘
```

Figure 3.4. Sign Up form Birth date section

The markup for this form section will look similar to this:

```html
<fieldset>
  <legend>Birth date</legend>
  <label for="dob_month">Month</label>
  <select name="dob_month" id="dob_month">
    <option> - Month - </option>
    ⋮ months …
  </select>

  <label for="dob_day">Day</label>
  <select name="dob_day" id="dob_day">
    <option> - Day - </option>
    ⋮ days …
  </select>

  <label for="dob_year">Year</label>
  <select name="dob_year" id="dob_year">
    <option> - Year - </option>
    ⋮ years …
  </select>
```

```
    <em class="note">This is hidden by default
        from your profile.</em>
</fieldset>
```

This technique will also be useful on the **Edit Profile** form.

There's another important aspect of our form design that we'll need to address, however: label usage. Consider the Advanced Search form shown in Figure 3.5. This form consists of two `select` elements, and contains a text box for the search terms.

Advanced Search

Search for [All of these words ÷] [   ]
Search in [People ÷]
(Search)

Figure 3.5. Advanced Search form

Both of the `select` elements will have an appropriate label on them in approximately the same way as the following markup:

```
<label for="words">Search for</label>
<select id="words" name="words">
  <option>All of these words</option>
  <option>Any of these words</option>
</select>

<input type="text" name="keywords" value="" id="keywords"/>

<label for="searchin">Search in</label>
<select id="searchin" name="searchin">
  <option>People</option>
  <option>Places</option>
  <option>Sports</option>
</select>
```

Did you notice the odd one out? The text field for search terms, with an `id` of `terms`, has no label of its own in the design. It's clear from looking at the design that the text field's purpose is implied because it's grouped with the `select` above it. But without a visual cue, how can you tell?

It's hardly a good idea to leave the `label` out for this field. Without a `label`, assistive technology like a screen reader will need to guess what the field is about; when the user tabs to the field, it has to announce *something* to the user. In the absence of a `label`, many screen readers will grab text near the field, sometimes with the unfortunate consequence that irrelevant, unrelated text is interpreted as the label for the form field.

So how do we solve this issue? The easiest solution is to use a label for every form field. In the case of our **Advanced Search** form, it would be simple enough to add in a label for the middle field for search terms. If the designer in you cringes from the idea of adding more visual clutter, have no fear—CSS allows us to hide the label in a number of ways. One popular technique is to use CSS to position the `label` a long way to the left of the field—so far left that it disappears beyond the left-most boundary of the page. You'll find a discussion of this method, and other text hiding techniques, at WebAIM.[3]

If using a `label` is simply impractical, most screen readers do also announce the `title` attribute on a form element. This is particularly useful if, for example, your fields are arranged in a table. When browsing a table, a screen reader will ordinarily announce the contents of the table's headings—the `th` element—as the user moves through each table cell. However, when a screen reader is in forms mode, those table headers are ignored; in this case, use the `title` attribute as a fallback. It's hardly an ideal option—a `label` is still best—but it at least provides some text for screen readers. You can find out more about this technique in Jim Thatcher's accessible forms tutorial.[4]

---

[3] http://www.webaim.org/techniques/css/invisiblecontent/
[4] http://jimthatcher.com/webcourse8.htm

Form Fields

The choices you have for form fields are fairly standard: text fields, password fields, radio buttons, checkboxes, drop-down lists (`select` elements), textareas, hidden fields, and buttons. The humble `<input/>` tag does the heavy lifting for most of those field types by simply changing its `type` attribute. In addition, the `<textarea></textarea>` and `<select></select>` tags, with one or more `<option></option>` tags, are also used. Forms are basically just a collection of these kinds of fields that are interrelated. Where it becomes fancy is in the way that we bring them together to create a whole, interactive experience.

In every form field element there are two essential attributes, `id` and `name`. The `id` attribute can be used as an identifier by CSS and JavaScript, but it's also required by the `for` attribute on your labels; it's what connects the labels to the form fields. The `name` attribute is submitted along with the form, so that the field value can be identified from other field values. Consider the following excerpt from the **Sign Up** form:

```
                                                    ch03/sign-up.html (excerpt)

<label for="email">Your email address</label>
<input type="text" name="email" id="email"/>
```

The email field is a `text` field, with the `name` email and the `id` email. The label is linked to the field because the `for` attribute value, `email`, matched the field's `id` value. When this form is submitted the data from this field will be represented as follows: email=*email_value*.

Of course, the `id` attribute must remain unique across all elements, but there are situations where more than one form field element can share the same `name`. One example is the use of radio buttons. Each radio button is implemented using a separate `<input/>` tag with the `type` value `radio`, and they're grouped by their `name` attribute. All the radio buttons with the `name` value are considered a group and only one button can be selected from a group. We'll make use of this feature in our **Privacy Settings** form.

Since this form is constructed as an HTML data table, we'll also take the opportunity to use the `title` attribute on each field, to ensure that our screen reader users will hear text at each field. The following code excerpt from that form demonstrates the use of the `name` and `title` attributes:

ch03/privacy-settings.html *(excerpt)*

```
  ⋮
<tr>
  <th>Gender</th>
  <td class="private">
    <input type="radio" name="gender" id="gender-private"
      value="private" title="Gender: private" checked="checked"/>
  </td>
  <td class="contacts">
    <input type="radio" name="gender" id="gender-contacts"
      value="contacts" title="Gender: contacts"/>
  </td>
  <td class="public">
    <input type="radio" name="gender" id="gender-public"
      value="public" title="Gender: public"/>
  </td>
</tr>
  ⋮
```

These radio buttons represent the chosen level of privacy for your gender information, where one of three levels can be selected: `private`, `contacts`, and `public`; `private` is checked by default. Even though they each have a unique `id` value, all three radio buttons share the same `name`: `gender`, which means the browser will only allow one of these three to be selected at any time. Notice also that they're placed in separate table cells; it's unnecessary for radio buttons to be grouped close together in your markup in order to function, they only have to share the same `name`. If the above form was submitted, the data from this field would be represented like so: `gender=private`.

There are a few other attributes of form fields that we have at our disposal: `tabindex`, `accesskey`, `readonly`, and `disabled` attributes are available for form fields, and all have a history of being used and abused in web forms.

tabindex specifies the order in which form fields take focus when a user tabs through the form. It's still available to use, though the more savvy practitioners have dropped it. Instead, I'd advise you to simply rely on the source order of your form to specify its natural flow. Following the general flow of the source is adequate for most forms.

`accesskey` has a long history of being used, and overused, in forms. The `accesskey` attribute provides a shortcut key that either activates or places the focus on the corresponding form field—the exact behavior depends on the browser. This technique, too, has fallen out of favor for a number of reasons: the difficulties of standardizing on a set of accesskeys, the lack of a mechanism to reliably override and/or redefine the keystrokes that the author specified, and the possibility that your choices may conflict with existing browser or other assistive technology keystrokes.

`disabled` and `read-only` form elements are visible but are unable to be edited, so are generally rendered in a fashion that suggest that they're faded or made gray. Using JavaScript, you can make these kinds of fields editable again—for example, you might choose to disable a particular form field until a previous question has been answered.

For more information about the different types of form fields see the SitePoint HTML Reference,[5] or, if you're adventurous, refer to the W3C's form documentation.[6] A great overview of creating forms is found in the SitePoint title *Build Your Own Web Site the Right Way Using HTML & CSS* (Melbourne: SitePoint, 2008) by Ian Lloyd—be sure to check it out if you're looking to understand all the basics!

Form Layout

Although not strictly the job of HTML, you may need to use additional markup to help you create the variety of form grid layouts required for your CSS to hook into. My preference is to use the generic `div` for defining a row of the form:

```
<div>
  <label for="email">Your email address</label>
  <input id="email" type="text" name="email" value=""/>
</div>
```

Individuals may advocate the use of list markup by suggesting that each form label and field pair is part of an ordered or unordered list's list item (`li`), or even that the label should be a `dt` and the field should be a `dd` of a definition list (`dl`). Others still may suggest that a table should be used when the form is a representation of tabular

---

[5] http://reference.sitepoint.com/html/elements-form/
[6] http://www.w3.org/TR/html4/interact/forms.html

data. If you build forms long enough, you too can enjoy these debates of semantic purity with others in the industry and colleagues at work! Actually, we do use an HTML table in one of our forms: the **Privacy Settings** form. A table is appropriate in this situation because those settings represent a two-dimensional option matrix.

Instructions, Errors, and Advisory Text

It's a rare form that requires no explanation. Most of the forms you'll make will require instructions, error text, and advisory text. How do we let the user know that certain fields are required? How do we help them understand what format an email address should be? How do we let them know that an error has occurred?

Required Fields

From time to time, you'll create a form where only some of the information is required, while other fields are optional. The easiest way to deal with required fields is to only ask for the data that's required. Eliminate all optional fields and your problem is solved—a simple statement saying all fields are required. Oh, if only it were that easy! We *do* need to provide some indication of required fields. So, with that in mind, what are our options?

Over the years certain conventions have become standard in web interfaces. In many cases, it seems that an asterisk is a fairly common way to denote a necessary field. Putting the asterisk on the page is the easy part. Where do we put it, though? And what do we do when required fields are skipped? Where should our error messages go? And how does an asterisk actually *mean* required, anyway? Let's take an in-depth look at what some best-practice markup should be for a few of these scenarios.

In cases where the asterisk will simply sit beside the text, it's clear that we should just include the asterisk in the label. It's the most semantically appropriate way to provide this information, and it helps screen reader users and potentially other users of assistive technology.

But what should we do when the design requires the asterisk be shown on the right-hand side of the field itself, rather than just to the right of the label? The fields in Figure 3.6 represent this kind of construction.

Username		*
Email Address		*
First Name		*
Last Name		*

Figure 3.6. Required fields indicated with an asterisk

When we think about this design in terms of a typical form grid, the asterisk is in a third column, sitting outside of where the form field's label is. Here's the problem: when the asterisk sits outside of the label it will remain unread by a screen reader, so a vital piece of information is omitted. Hence, we must ensure that the asterisk is contained within the label.

The solution lies in some creative use of markup and styles (we'll look more closely at the CSS techniques to achieve this in the next chapter):

```
<label for="username">Username
  <abbr title="Required field">*</abbr>
</label>

<input id="uname" type="text" name="uname" value=""/>
```

Placing the asterisk as part of the label ensures that it will be read out by a screen reader when its user interacts with the form. The use of the abbr element is also a nice semantic touch—after all, in the case of our form, the * really *is* an abbreviation for *Required Field*. Armed with this knowledge, we can now extend this pattern to ensure that we communicate error messages and advisory content to all users in a similar fashion.

The design of our Sign Up form, shown again in Figure 3.7, now includes three components that indicate an error has occurred: a red border around the troublesome field, an icon next to the field, and a message above the form to explain what the errors are.

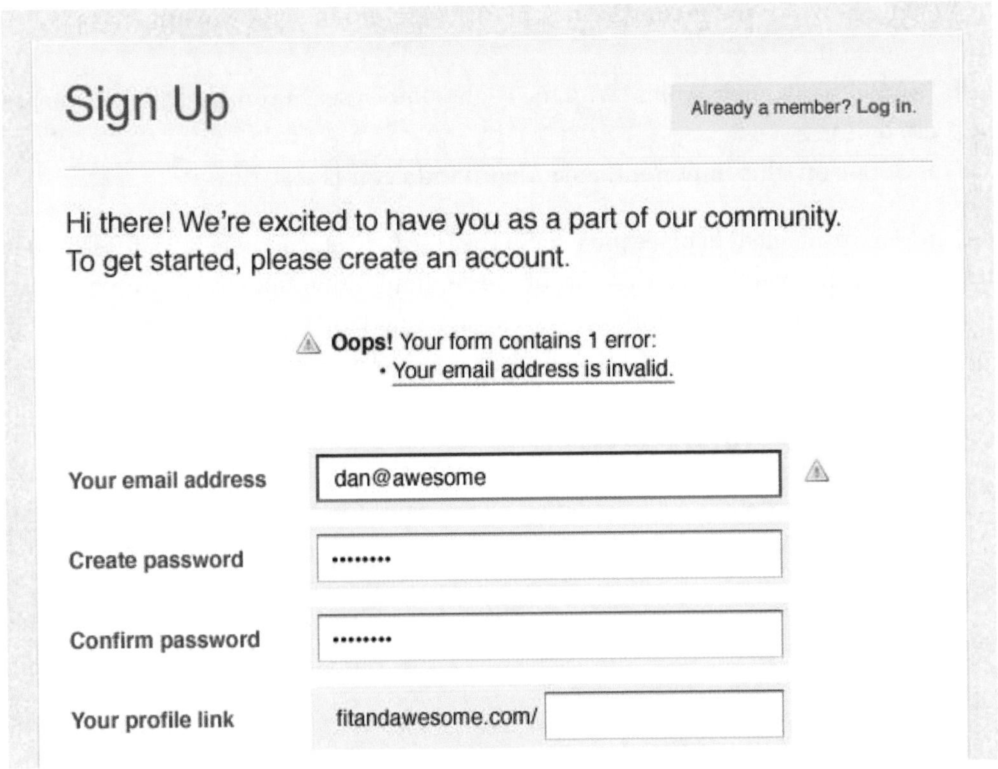

Sign Up

Already a member? Log in.

Hi there! We're excited to have you as a part of our community. To get started, please create an account.

⚠ **Oops!** Your form contains 1 error:
- Your email address is invalid.

Your email address   dan@awesome   ⚠

Create password   ••••••••

Confirm password   ••••••••

Your profile link   fitandawesome.com/

Figure 3.7. Errors are indicated with highlighting, an icon, and text

The markup for the field might look like this:

```
<label for="email">
  Your email address
  <strong>
    <img src="error.png" alt="Error"/>
  </strong>
</label>

<input id="email" type="text" name="email" value=""/>
```

You can see above that we've used an img element here. It's equally possible to add a class to the label, and then add that image as a background using CSS. But beware, this can cause more problems than it solves:

- Some browsers are unable to magnify background images when the page is zoomed in.
- In a Windows environment with the High Contrast setting on, background images are omitted.
- If CSS is off, this important, meaningful indicator is lost.

Using an img element to place the icon in the HTML itself counters all of these issues and establishes iconography as part of the content, rather than the presentation. In doing so we can ensure that the importance of that icon in communication is conveyed, regardless of the technology that the site visitor is using for their experience.[7]

The Final Markup

Taking into consideration all the points we've raised in this chapter we can now produce the HTML for our forms. All of our forms will use this basic structure:

```
<h1>Form Heading</h1>
<form action="#" method="post">
  <fieldset>
    <p>Introductory paragraph</p>

    : form body …

  </fieldset>
</form>
```

We'll wrap all the form fields within a fieldset element, but avoid adding a legend. The form heading is placed before the opening <form> tag, and if required, an introductory paragraph can be added using a p element.

Within the form body we'll use div elements to separate the individual fields—in a sense making "rows"—like so:

---

[7] For more information about wrongly chosen background images—I've griped about this earlier—check out *Naughty or Nice? CSS Background Images*, located at http://24ways.org/2005/naughty-or-nice-css-background-images

```
<div>
  <label for="id">field label</label>
  ⋮ field …
</div>
```

An exception to this will be our **Privacy Settings** form, where we'll use an HTML table.

There are cases where we'll use a `fieldset` and `legend` element within our main form body to indicate a subsection of the form, like so:

```
<fieldset>
  ⋮ form body …

  <div>
    <fieldset>
      <legend>subsection name</legend>
      ⋮ subsection fields …
    </fieldset>
  </div>

  ⋮ form body …
</fieldset>
```

In situations where a field is required we indicate the requirement like so:

```
<div>
  <label for="id">field label
    <abbr title="Required field">*</abbr>
  </label>
  ⋮ field …
</div>
```

To indicate a validation error we'll use the follow markup:

```
<div>
  <label for="id">field label
    <strong><img src="error.gif" alt="Error"/></strong>
  </label>
  ⋮ field …
</div>
```

The last element of all our forms will be the form submit control. This will be placed at the end of the form body, within a div element that has a class value of controls, like so:

```
: form body …
<div class="controls">
  <input id="submit" name="submit" type="submit"
      value="submit button text"/>
</div>
  </fieldset>
</form>
```

Here are our completed forms:

Sign Up form

```html
<h1>Sign Up</h1>
<p class="log-in">Already a member? <a href="#">Log in</a>.</p>
<form action="#" method="post">
  <fieldset>
    <p class="introduction">Hi there! We're excited to have you as
        a part of our community. To get started, please create an
        account.</p>
    <p class="note">Fields marked with an asterisk (<abbr title=
        "Required field">*</abbr>) are required.</p>
    <!-- Email -->
    <div>
      <label for="email">Your email address
        <abbr title="Required field">*</abbr></label>
      <input type="text" name="email" id="email"/>
    </div>

    <!-- Password -->
    <div>
      <label for="password">Create Password
        <abbr title="Required field">*</abbr></label>
      <input type="password" name="password" id="password"/>
    </div>

    <!-- Password Confirmation -->
    <div>
      <label for="password_confirmation">Confirm Password
        <abbr title="Required field">*</abbr></label>
      <input type="password" name="password_confirmation"
          id="password_confirmation"/>
    </div>

    <!-- Profile Link -->
    <div id="field-profile-link">
      <label for="profile_link">Your profile link
        <abbr title="Required field">*</abbr></label>
      <span class="profile-link-prefix">fitandawesome.com/</span>
      <input type="text" name="profile_link" id="profile_link"/>
    </div>

    <!-- DOB -->
```

```
<fieldset id="section-dob" class="group">
<legend><span>Birth date</span></legend>
  <!-- Month -->
  <div>
    <label for="dob_month">Month</label>
    <select name="dob_month" id="dob_month">
      <option value=""> - Month - </option>
      ⋮ months
    </select>
  </div>

  <!-- Day -->
  <div>
    <label for="dob_day">Day</label>
    <select name="dob_day" id="dob_day">
      <option value=""> - Day - </option>
      <option value="1">1</option>
      ⋮ days
    </select>
  </div>

  <!-- Year -->
  <div>
    <label for="dob_year">Year</label>
    <select name="dob_year" id="dob_year">
      <option value=""> - Year - </option>
      <option value="2004">2004</option>
      ⋮ years
    </select>
  </div>
  <em class="note">This is hidden by default from your
      profile.</em>
</fieldset>

<!-- Terms of Service -->
<div id="field-agree-tos">
  <ul>
    <li>
      <label for="agree_tos">
        <input type="checkbox" id="agree_tos"
            name="agree_tos" value="yes"/>
        I have read and agree to the <a href="#">Terms
            of Service</a>.
      </label>
```

```
        </li>
      </ul>
    </div>

    <!-- Controls -->
    <div class="controls">
      <input id="submit" name="submit" type="submit"
         value="Create Profile"/>
    </div>
  </fieldset>
</form>
```

Advanced Search form

ch03/advanced-search.html *(excerpt)*

```html
<h1>Advanced Search</h1>
<form action="#" method="get">
  <fieldset>
    <!-- Search for: -->
    <div>
     <label for="words">Search for</label>
     <select id="words" name="words">
       <option>All of these words</option>
       <option>Any of these words</option>
     </select>

     <input type="text" name="keywords" value="" id="keywords"/>

    </div>

    <!-- Search in -->
    <div>
     <label for="searchin">Search in</label>

     <select id="searchin" name="searchin">
       <option>People</option>
       <option>Places</option>
       <option>Sports</option>
     </select>
    </div>


    <!-- Controls -->
    <div class="controls">
     <input id="submit" name="submit" type="submit"
        value="Search"/>
    </div>
  </fieldset>
</form>
```

Change Password form

```html
<h1>Change Password</h1>
<form action="#" method="get">
  <fieldset>
    <!-- Current -->
    <div>
     <label for="current">Current password</label>
      <input type="password" name="current" value=""
         id="current"/>
    </div>

    <!-- New -->
    <div>
     <label for="new">New password</label>
      <input type="password" name="new" value="" id="new"/>
    </div>

    <!-- Confirm -->
    <div>
     <label for="confirm">Confirm password</label>
      <input type="password" name="confirm" value=""
         id="confirm"/>
    </div>

    <!-- Controls -->
    <div class="controls">
     <input id="submit" name="submit" type="submit"
         value="Change password"/>
    </div>
  </fieldset>
</form>
```

Edit Profile form

```
<h1>Edit Profile</h1>
<form action="#" method="post">
  <fieldset>
    <!-- photo -->
    <div>
      <label for="your_photo">Your profile photo</label>
      <input type="file" name="your_photo" value=""
          id="your_photo"/>
    </div>

    <!-- first name -->
    <div>
      <label for="firstname">First name</label>
      <input type="text" name="firstname" value=""
          id="firstname"/>
    </div>

    <!-- last name -->
    <div>
      <label for="lastname">Last name</label>
      <input type="text" name="lastname" value=""
          id="lastname"/>
    </div>

    <!-- gender -->
    <div>
      <fieldset id="gender" class="">
        <legend>Gender</legend>
        <label for="female">Female</label>
        <input type="radio" name="gender" value="female"
            id="female"/>
        <label for="male">Male</label>
        <input type="radio" name="gender" value="male"
            id="male"/>
      </fieldset>
    </div>
    <!-- DOB -->
    <fieldset id="section-dob" class="group">
    <legend><span>Birth date</span></legend>
      <!-- Month -->
```

```
<div>
  <label for="dob_month">Month</label>
  <select name="dob_month" id="dob_month">
    <option value=""> - Month - </option>
    ⋮ months
  </select>
</div>

<!-- Day -->
<div>
  <label for="dob_day">Day</label>
  <select name="dob_day" id="dob_day">
    <option value=""> - Day - </option>
    <option value="1">1</option>
    ⋮ days
  </select>
</div>

<!-- Year -->
<div>
  <label for="dob_year">Year</label>
  <select name="dob_year" id="dob_year">
    <option value=""> - Year - </option>
    <option value="2004">2004</option>
    ⋮ years
  </select>
</div>
<em class="note">This is hidden by default from your
    profile.</em>
</fieldset>


<!-- about you -->
<div>
  <label for="about_you">About you</label>
  <textarea name="about_you" id="about_you" cols="30"
    rows="6"></textarea>
</div>

<!-- website url -->
<div>
  <label for="website_url">Website URL</label>
  <input type="text" name="website_url" value=""
    id="website_url"/>
```

```
    </div>

    <!-- website name -->
    <div>
      <label for="website_name">Website name</label>
      <input type="text" name="website_url" value=""
          id="website_name"/>
    </div>
    <!-- Controls -->
     <div class="controls">
      <input id="submit" name="submit" type="submit"
      value="Create Profile"/>
     </div>
  </fieldset>
</form>
```

Feedback form

```html
<h1>Feedback</h1>
<form action="#" method="post">
  <fieldset>
    <p class="introduction">Tell us what you think about the site.
       What is working for you? What would you like to see
       inproved? Your opinion is very valuable to us. <strong>All
       fields are required.</strong></p>
    <!-- Your Name -->
    <div>
      <label for="name">Your name
        <abbr title="Required field">*</abbr>
      </label>
      <input type="text" name="name" id="name"/>
    </div>

    <!-- Email -->
    <div>
      <label for="email">Your email address</label>
      <input type="text" name="email" id="email"/>
    </div>

    <!-- Password -->
    <div>
      <label for="comment">Your comments</label>
      <textarea name="comment" id="comment" cols="30" rows="6">
      </textarea>
    </div>

    <!-- Controls -->
    <div class="controls">
      <input id="submit" name="submit" type="submit"
          value="Submit Feedback"/>
    </div>
  </fieldset>
</form>
```

Privacy Settings form

```
<h1>
  Privacy Settings
</h1>
<form action="#" method="get">
  <fieldset>
    <p class="introduction">
      We understand that your health and fitness is personal. We
      respect your privacy. Please let us know what you would
      like to be visible.
    </p>
    <table summary="Profile visibility settings">
      <thead>
        <tr>
          <th scope="row"></th>
          <th abbr="Keep private" class="private" scope="col">
            Private
          </th>
          <th abbr="Show only to contacts" class="contacts"
            scope="col">
            Contacts
          </th>
          <th abbr="Show publicly" class="public" scope="col">
            Public
          </th>
        </tr>
      </thead>
      <tbody>
        <tr>
          <th scope="row">
            Gender
          </th>
          <td class="private">
            <input type="radio" name="gender"
              id="gender-private" value="private"
              title="Gender: private"
              checked="checked"/>
          </td>
          <td class="contacts">
            <input type="radio" name="gender"
              id="gender-contacts" value="contacts"
```

```
          title="Gender: contacts"/>
      </td>
      <td class="public">
        <input type="radio" name="gender"
          id="gender-public" value="public"
          title="Gender: public"/>
      </td>
    </tr>
    <tr>
      <th scope="row">
        Birth day and month
      </th>
      <td class="private">
        <input type="radio" name="dob_date"
          id="dob-date-private" value="private"
          title="Birth day: private"
          checked="checked"/>
      </td>
      <td class="contacts">
        <input type="radio" name="dob_date"
          id="dob-date-contacts" value="contacts"
          title="Birth day: contacts"/>
      </td>
      <td class="public">
        <input type="radio" name="dob_date"
          id="dob-date-public" value="public"
          title="Birth day: public"/>
      </td>
    </tr>
    <tr>
      <th scope="row">
        Birth year
      </th>
      <td class="private">
        <input type="radio" name="dob_year"
          id="dob-year-private" value="private"
          title="Birth year: private"
          checked="checked"/>
      </td>
      <td class="contacts">
        <input type="radio" name="dob_year"
          id="dob-year-contacts" value="contacts"
          title="Birth year: contacts"/>
      </td>
```

```
      <td class="public">
        <input type="radio" name="dob_year"
          id="dob-year-public" value="public"
          title="Birth year: public"/>
      </td>
    </tr>
    <tr>
      <th scope="row">
        Location
      </th>
      <td class="private">
        <input type="radio" name="location"
          id="location-private" value="private"
          title="Location: private"
          checked="checked"/>
      </td>
      <td class="contacts">
        <input type="radio" name="location"
          id="location-contacts" value="contacts"
          title="Location: contacts"/>
      </td>
      <td class="public">
        <input type="radio" name="location"
          id="location-public" value="public"
          title="Location: public"/>
      </td>
    </tr>
    <tr class="with-note">
      <th scope="row">
        Fitness journal entries
      </th>
      <td class="private">
        <input type="radio" name="entries"
          id="entries-private" value="private"
          title="Journal: private"
          checked="checked"/>
      </td>
      <td class="contacts">
        <input type="radio" name="entries"
          id="entries-contacts" value="contacts"
          title="Journal: contacts"/>
      </td>
      <td class="public">
        <input type="radio" name="entries"
```

```
        id="entries-public" value="public"
        title="Journal: public"/>
  </td>
</tr>
<tr>
  <th scope="row"></th>
  <td colspan="3" class="note">
    This can be changed on a post-by-post basis.
  </td>
</tr>
<tr class="with-note">
  <th scope="row">
    Your photos
  </th>
  <td class="private">
    <input type="radio" name="photos"
      id="photos-private" value="private"
      title="Notes: private"
      checked="checked"/>
  </td>
  <td class="contacts">
    <input type="radio" name="photos"
      id="photos-contacts" value="contacts"
      title="Notes: contacts"/>
  </td>
  <td class="public">
    <input type="radio" name="photos"
      id="photos-public" value="public"
      title="Notes: public"/>
  </td>
</tr>
<tr>
  <th scope="row"></th>
  <td colspan="3" class="note">
    This can be changed on a post-by-post basis.
  </td>
</tr>
<tr>
  <th scope="row">
    Your fitness stats
  </th>
  <td class="private">
    <input type="radio" name="stats"
      id="stats-private" value="private"
```

```
              title="Stats: private"
              checked="checked"/>
        </td>
        <td class="contacts">
          <input type="radio" name="stats"
            id="stats-contacts" value="contacts"
            title="Stats: contacts"/>
        </td>
        <td class="public">
          <input type="radio" name="stats"
            id="stats-public" value="public"
            title="Stats: public"/>
        </td>
      </tr>
    </tbody>
  </table>
  <div class="controls">
    <input id="submit" name="submit" type="submit"
      value="Update Settings"/>
  </div>
  </fieldset>
</form>
```

Conclusion

I know you're more than ready to dive into creating your form's layout and visual design, but the time we've spent here considering the HTML structure of our form is time well spent. We've carefully considered our use of `fieldset`, `legend`, and `label` elements, how to build a structure that will support our layout requirements, and how we'll communicate field information and errors.

The solid HTML foundation we established in this chapter will ensure that your beautiful forms are also functional and accessible to all of your web site visitors. The final two chapters will see your forms take shape, so what are you waiting for?

Styling

Almost every new front-end web developer I've ever spoken to seems to draw the same conclusion I did when beginning to learn CSS: forms are very, very tricky to style! There are a lot of complex elements involved here. We have text input boxes of two varieties (the input fields and the textareas). There are select menus of two varieties: single item select menus and multiple item select menus. We have radio buttons, checkboxes, labels, fieldsets, legends, buttons ... all sorts of components that can require a lot more effort than your typical paragraph or heading—especially if the design is highly customized. And to top it all off, it seems that every single browser renders these elements completely differently!

Making form elements appear consistent in every browser is, in my opinion, one of the most challenging CSS problems to solve. So how do you achieve this?

Well, the first question to ask is: do you really need to achieve this? Yes, this is a book called *Fancy Form Design*, and why would we deter you from anything other than fancy-looking forms? But we do want you to understand certain implications first before diving in—and it's important to remember that even if you're stuck with the native styles of your browser, you can still achieve a fairly fancy form.

Stuff to Consider

By now, after all this planning, designing, and construction, you're probably anxious to start styling. Usability and technical considerations are definitely important, and should be in your mind throughout the entire process; that means we need to think about those issues now, as well as in your initial phases.

There are both technical and usability concerns that should be carefully considered and thought-out when styling form elements.

The first aspect to consider is your audience. What do they expect? Are they a really tech-savvy audience? Great—bust out the fancy stuff! Your spiffy, trend-setting, super-customized form widget from the future will probably *ooh and aah* them to your amusement and satisfaction! What if your audience is less technically inclined, or has a broader range of skill levels? Well … you might want to tone it down a bit.

Of course, some of these issues should have already been considered in the planning and designing phase; however, we've found that certain factors only surface when you start building the forms.

Then, on the technical side: how feasible is it to bring your design to life, really? Yes, you may have seen some pretty effect or technique used elsewhere, but is it worth going to the trouble if a certain feature is ridiculously laborious to build? Sometimes it's worth altering the original design or concept a bit to make development that much easier—or at least modifying your expectations. Your lovely CSS effects might look stunning in Firefox 3, but if it is impossible to recreate them in Internet Explorer 6, you are probably justified in providing a slightly less fancy experience to users of that browser.

But we can certainly try to create a usable experience in as many browsers as possible, without handicapping the experience in other browsers. This is the key factor to remember as you continue on in this book. Of course, we want fanciness, but we're practical.

Preparing Your Canvas

A common approach adopted by modern web developers is to begin with a consistent (as possible) canvas across browsers (as distinct from the canvas element in HTML). Some developers disagree with this for various reasons—all legitimate, but it's an approach we prefer to take. The motivation here is that while some developers might think of a default web page (with no explicit CSS applied to it in any way) as "unstyled," it actually *is* styled. That's because browsers have their own built-in style sheets that determine how even the default appearance of HTML elements will appear.

If you think about the body element, for example, it's common practice to set the margin and padding to zero so that there's no gap around the edge of the viewport. What we're doing here is overriding the styles that the browser has automatically integrated into its engine that puts that gap there in the first place. Each browser has its own way of displaying defaults because each browser has its own integrated and unique style sheet.

When creating a consistent canvas, you may also potentially be overriding user style sheets. Some users will create their own default style sheet that they import or set within the browser so that elements appear the way they prefer. While you may find it preferable (from a designer's perspective) to override a user's style sheet to achieve the desired appearance, keep in mind that some of those styles may be there for accessibility reasons. Be considerate of the user's needs.

Here are a couple of approaches to co-exist happily with user style sheets:

1. Use what's known as a **CSS signature** in your markup—add an `id` to your `body` element, such as `#fit-and-awesome`, which gives a stylesheet-savvy user a hook to control your site's appearance in their custom styles. This technique's name was coined by Eric Meyer.[1]
2. Avoid using the `!important` declaration, which can wreak havoc on a user's custom styles.

---

[1] http://archivist.incutio.com/viewlist/css-discuss/13291

Reset Styles

When we talk about **resetting** styles, we mean that we're using a set of declarations to override (reset) the browser's built-in style sheet, and then add styles back.

Because developers differ in their opinion on what should be reset or stay intact, there have been a few implementations of a CSS reset released. Here are some of the common ones used currently.

The Global Whitespace Reset

The global whitespace reset, documented by Andrew Krespanis,[2] was a technique previously used in all my projects until about a couple years ago. This small and simple snippet removes the margin and padding on all elements—every single element on the page, both inline and block level. It's short and it's sweet, as seen below:

```
* {
  padding: 0;
  margin: 0;
}
```

Some people prefer it because it's very quick and convenient: it enables you to avoid declaring each and every element that ought to have the whitespace removed. However, some developers avoid it out of concern that it may cause usability issues, particularly in regards to browser UI elements.[3]

Tantek Çelik's undohtml.css

Tantek's undohtml.css[4] was one of the first reset style sheets we encountered that took care of more than just margins and padding.

We like this approach because it includes typical behaviors we find ourselves doing in our own development work, plus Tantek also took the time to explain what the rules are for. If you were to use this, you might consider removing his comments for optimization—of course, you should leave his Creative Commons license intact!

---

[2] http://leftjustified.net/journal/2004/10/19/global-ws-reset/

[3] http://www.kurafire.net/log/archive/2005/07/26/starting-css-revisited

[4] http://tantek.com/log/2004/09.html#d06t2354

Yahoo UI Library's Reset CSS

Yahoo has produced its own Reset CSS file[5] that's also included in the Yahoo CSS library. There's even a hosted version of the file so that you can import or link directly to it. It's well-commented and reasonably thorough.

Eric Meyer's Reset CSS

Eric Meyer created a reset style sheet[6] that has since been integrated into many of today's CSS frameworks—the most commonly known example would be the seemingly controversial BluePrint CSS framework.[7] We'll be using a customized version of this reset style sheet.

Meyer's reset style sheet wipes out all margins, padding, borders, and outlines of essentially every HTML element, with the exception of form elements. This latter exception is motivated by the previously mentioned notion that resetting margins and padding on form elements can cause usability problems.

Here's the customized reset style sheet we'll be using for the rest of this book, which includes much of Meyer's work, and introduces some additional handy defaults that suit our design:

ch04/css/reset.css (excerpt)

```
html, body, blockquote, pre, abbr, acronym, address, code,
em, img, dl, dt, dd, ol, ul, li,
fieldset, form, label, legend,
table, caption, tbody, tfoot, thead, tr, th, td {
  margin: 0;
  padding: 0;
  border: 0;
  vertical-align: baseline;
}
```

---

[5] http://developer.yahoo.com/yui/reset/

[6] http://meyerweb.com/eric/tools/css/reset/

[7] CSS frameworks are certainly a polarizing topic—for an example of some hot debate, see Jeff Croft's post, *What's So Bad About CSS Frameworks*, and the attendant discussion at http://jeffcroft.com/blog/2007/nov/17/whats-not-love-about-css-frameworks/

```
ul {
  list-style: none;
}

table { border-collapse: separate; border-spacing: 0; }
caption, th, td { text-align: left; font-weight: normal; }
table, td, th { vertical-align: middle; }

blockquote:before, blockquote:after, q:before, q:after
  { content: ""; }
blockquote, q { quotes: "" ""; }

a img { border: none; }
```

Build a Framework

As developers grow in skill, patterns begin to emerge. Take a look at the interfaces you've styled in the past, and you'll no doubt see patterns to your work. This is particularly true for the world of forms—there are only so many ways a form can be laid out, and the more forms you create, the more you'll feel a little *déjà vu* surrounding the process.

Why not put together a collection of snippets to form your very own framework to speed up your styling? Coupled with the perfect markup for forms, such frameworks can make for rapid styling, allowing you to concentrate on making those forms even fancier. You'll soon find yourself with more time to spend on planning, designing, and enhancing your form.

As you make your way through this chapter, feel free to grab a copy of the code archive to peruse, admire, criticize, and adapt the examples. Use them as a basis for your very own framework of layouts and styles. Once you have your own framework, hold it close and never let it go.

Fieldsets and Legends

Some of the trickiest form elements to style are the `fieldset` and `legend`. Each browser brings its own ideas to the table, with wildly varying results that can prove to be downright frustrating. Adjusting the size, color, and font of legends will normally behave as expected—that is, just like adjusting text on any other element; but as soon as positioning and layout enter the picture, the story changes. Below, in Figure 4.1, you'll see a fairly standard example of how a browser renders a `fieldset` and `legend`.

Sign Up

Lorem ipsum dolor sit amet, consectetuer adipiscing elit. Donec odio. Quisque volutpat mattis eros. Nullam malesuada erat ut turpis. Suspendisse urna nibh, viverra non, semper suscipit, posuere a, pede.

Figure 4.1. Your garden variety `fieldset` and `legend`

The good news is that with a little trickery and wit, we can tame those pesky elements: enter an inventive use of the `span` element. Wrap that baby around the text within your `legend`, and suddenly, your misbehaving `legend` element becomes a model citizen once more:

```
<fieldset>
  <legend><span>My legend</span></legend>
  ⋮ fields …
<fieldset>
```

Clutter and Semantics

Some developers believe that adding a `span` here and there to simplify your styling efforts is quite undesirable, as they're semantically meaningless. Unfortunately, the variance in browser behavior can mean you have very little choice. If you're anti-`span`, one way to have your cake and eat it too is to embrace progressive enhancement and include that markup with a little JavaScript. In the ever-popular jQuery, you'd add it like so:

```
$('legend').wrapInner('<span></span>');
```

Thinking of our own forms, we previously decided that we would use a heading in place of a `legend` for the main title of each form. This is both a solid semantic decision and a great way to make styling much simpler; however, there are still many situations when a `legend` element ought to be used. It's reasonably easy to ensure that they're styled to look like a heading.

Back in Figure 4.1, we saw a typical default styling of a `legend` and `fieldset` combination. This is fine for many forms, but we'll need to push the boundaries a little. Let's style up that `legend` to look more like a heading.

The key action we're performing here is to remove all borders from the `fieldset` so that our `legend` butts up against the left. A little absolute positioning also goes a long way to ensuring that we escape the general confines of default `legend` styling:

```css
fieldset {
  border: none;
  position: relative;
  padding: 70px 0 0;
}

fieldset legend span {
  border-bottom: 1px solid #fff;
  display: block;
  font-size: 2.25em;
  line-height: 1.1;
  margin: 20px 0;
  padding-bottom: 20px;
  position: absolute;
  width: 560px;
}
```

Keen observers may have noticed that our markup for the Sign Up form shown in Chapter 4 included a nested `fieldset`, which contains the three fields that comprise the Birth Date question. Let's revisit and style that one later on in the chapter once we have our general layout sorted.

Form Questions

The star of the show is finally here—it's time to style those form elements. With our well-structured, semantic markup, it's possible to lay out our form questions in many fancy ways. Here are some handy techniques to try.

Top-aligned Labels

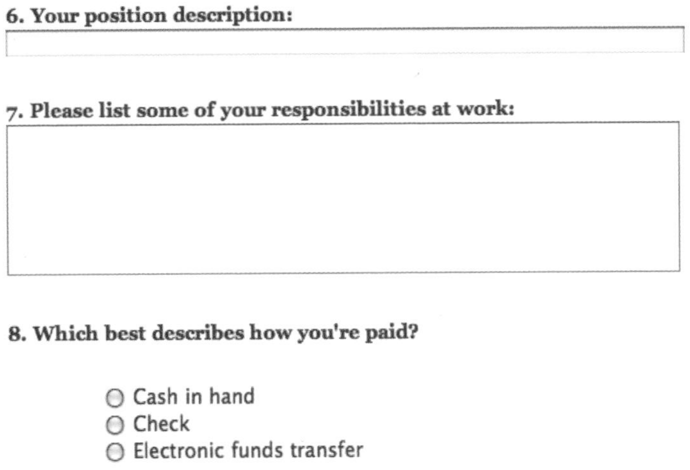

6. Your position description:

7. Please list some of your responsibilities at work:

8. Which best describes how you're paid?

- ○ Cash in hand
- ○ Check
- ○ Electronic funds transfer

Figure 4.2. These labels are aligned above the fields

Top-aligned labels, such as those seen in Figure 4.2, can make for great form readability. When aligning labels and form elements from top to bottom in one line, the user can easily cast their eyes down and through the form. This is because there is little resistance in eye movement, minimizing that left-to-right darting movement required to read a columned layout.

Many designers resist top-aligned labels to try to save on space and create an illusion of a shorter, less daunting form. While many simpler forms benefit from economical use of space, on longer or more complex forms, it's hard to resist the benefits of top-aligned labels. Such forms often feature longer questions, which can make it difficult to squeeze all that text into a column to the left, and can require wide input fields for answers.

If it is a top-aligned label you need, here is some CSS to accomplish exactly that:

```
label {
  display: block;
}

input,
textarea,
select {
  display: block;
}
```

Simple.

Side-by-side Labels

Perhaps you want to make that form appear shorter and less daunting, and generally a little more appealing. One way to do that is to align your labels to the left, and your fields to the right—like the ones in our mockups for Fit and Awesome. It's a common arrangement for shorter forms, and a simple way to accomplish this is through negative margins.

 When Floats Don't Float Your Boat

Floats are by no means the only way to arrange elements side by side. We have used negative margins over floats in the above code to avoid common cross-browser issues. Check out *Smashing Magazine*'s Definitive Guide to Negative Margins[8] for a good overview of how this technique works.

Another interesting option here is to try out a CSS table layout, using CSS's table display options. Find out about CSS table display at the W3C,[9] or pick up the book, *Everything You Know About CSS is Wrong!* written by Kevin Yank and Rachel Andrew (Melbourne: SitePoint, 2008).

Here, we'll apply a margin to the left of our rows and pull the label over with a negative margin:

---

[8] http://www.smashingmagazine.com/2009/07/27/the-definitive-guide-to-using-negative-margins/
[9] http://www.w3.org/TR/CSS2/tables.html

```
fieldset div {
  margin: 0 0 10px 160px;
}

fieldset div label {
  line-height: 1.1;
  margin: 5px 20px 0 -160px;
  width: 140px;
  float: left;
}

fieldset div input,
fieldset div textarea,
fieldset div select {
  display: block;
  line-height: 1;
}
```

It can be quite pleasing to have your form's labels right-justified and inputs left-justified, so that there's a nice vertical rhythm. It's as simple as adding a `text-align` declaration to the `label` elements in our code above:

```
fieldset div label {
    ⋮
  text-align: right;
}
```

The Trouble with Widgets

With our general structure in place, it's time to deal with the finer details of our form styling: the form widgets themselves.

We already know that each browser and operating system brings its own little flair to the game. In Figure 4.3 through to Figure 4.6, we can see some examples of how form elements can appear in just a few browsers and operating systems.

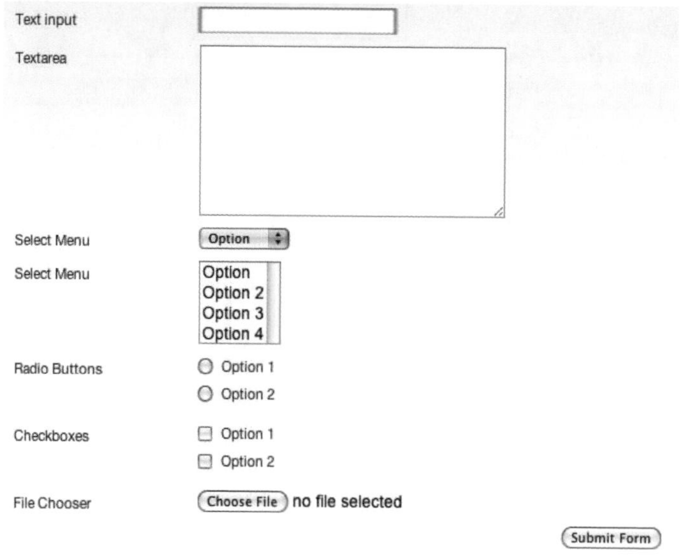

Text input

Textarea

Select Menu   Option

Select Menu   Option
                     Option 2
                     Option 3
                     Option 4

Radio Buttons   ○ Option 1
                     ○ Option 2

Checkboxes   ☐ Option 1
                     ☐ Option 2

File Chooser   (Choose File) no file selected

                                      (Submit Form)

Figure 4.3. Glossy Mac-style widgets, as seen in Safari

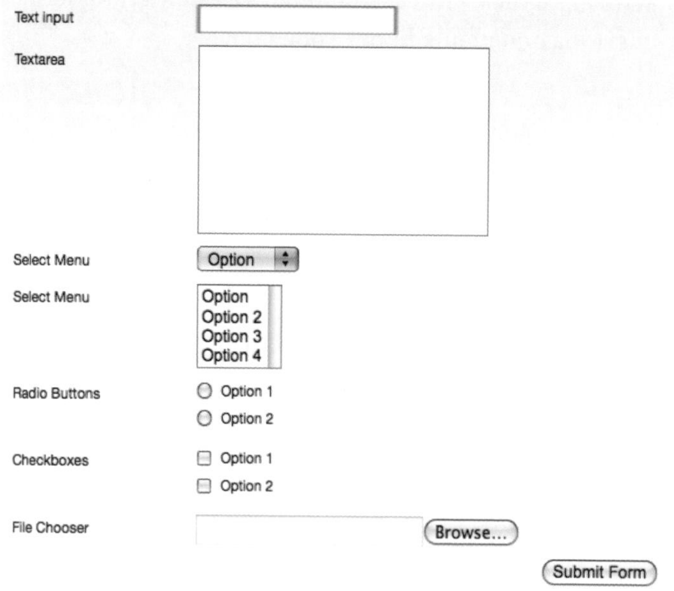

Text input

Textarea

Select Menu   Option

Select Menu   Option
                     Option 2
                     Option 3
                     Option 4

Radio Buttons   ○ Option 1
                     ○ Option 2

Checkboxes   ☐ Option 1
                     ☐ Option 2

File Chooser   (Browse...)

                                      (Submit Form)

Figure 4.4. Still glossy, but slightly different in Firefox 3 for the Mac

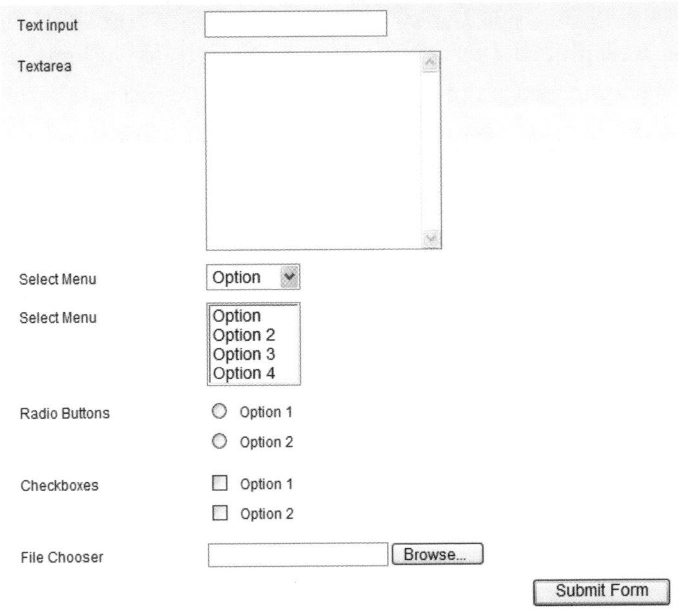

Figure 4.5. Widgets in Internet Explorer 7: rather blue

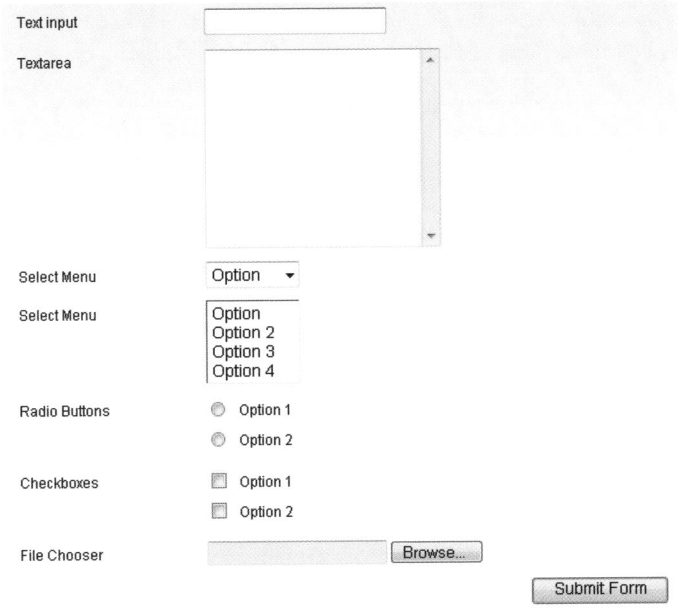

Figure 4.6. Widgets in Internet Explorer 8: same size, different color

The short version of the story is that there are no specifications for form element styling, and as a result browser manufacturers generally style their elements to re-semble interface widgets from the native operating system. Some call it a consistent operating system experience—others call it downright frustrating!

The Good News is ...

Feeling concerned by all that talk of browser inconsistency? Here's a good news story to make us all feel a little cheerier. In most cases, as soon as one applies a border to a text `input` or `textarea`, the browser-imposed native styling of these elements will disappear. Below is a quick recipe for some simple, clean text fields:

```
input,
textarea {
  border: 1px solid #666666;
  padding: 5px;
  width: 220px;
}

textarea {
  height: 140px;
}
```

And in Figure 4.7, here's the result:

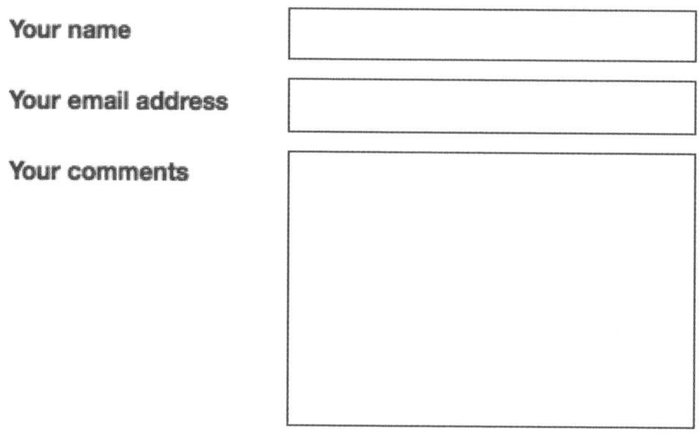

Figure 4.7. Some tidy textareas

Unexpected Side Effects

When styling input elements broadly, as above, remember to undo those changes for checkboxes and radio buttons—otherwise they'll acquire some unattractive borders, as Figure 4.8 attests.

Radio Buttons	⦿	Option 1
	○	Option 2
Checkboxes	☐	Option 1
	☐	Option 2

Figure 4.8. Whoops ...

If you're placing your boxes and radio buttons into a list, try overriding the effect with a `border: none` declaration, like this:

```
ul li input {
  border: none;
}
```

You may also want to reset any margins, paddings, and backgrounds previously applied to inputs as well.

Now that we've removed native browser styling, there are some fun effects we can apply to these elements. Let's explore some!

A Little Gradient Goes a Long Way

A subtle gradient can add some pop to flat and tedious textareas. Let's add a small repeating gradient along the width of our form elements, and lighten the border a little to enhance our simplistic styling above:

```
input,
textarea {
  ⋮
  background: url(css/images/bg-input-gradient.png) repeat-x 0 0;
}
```

Voilà! We can now see a little depth in those text entry fields, shown in Figure 4.9.

Your name

Your email address

Your comments

Figure 4.9. A little shadow adds depth

Visual Hints with Icons

Perhaps some iconography can help! Icons placed into the background of a text input field can emphasize the purpose of the field, as well as add a touch of fun. Let's experiment with that—we'll enhance a contact details form by adding icons to represent a person, an email address, and a comment.

There are oodles of royalty-free icons out there on the Web. We've grabbed a set called Web Application Icon Set from over at WebAppers[10] and made a set of CSS sprites, depicted in Figure 4.10.

Figure 4.10. Person, email, and comment icons in grayscale and color

[10] http://www.webappers.com/2008/02/12/webappers-released-free-web-application-icons-set/

Sprites?

Sprites are a fantastic way to add some speed to the way background images work. If you find you're using numerous background images as icons, highlights, or decorations, that normally means creating background image files for each one, all of which must be requested separately by the browser. Using the sprites technique, your background images are all combined into a single image, and CSS's `background-position` property is used to control which part of the image is shown for each element. One larger image is faster for the user to download than multiple individual images, since only one HTTP request is made by the browser. Dave Shea's article for A List Apart explains the technique in detail.[11]

Now, we'll use the `background-position` property to reveal the appropriate portion of the sprite as the background for each of the fields. The fields will also require some padding to their left, so that there's no overlap between the text and the image:

```
input#name,
input#email,
textarea#comment {
  background: url(css/images/bg-input-icons.png) no-repeat 3px 0;
  padding: 5px 5px 5px 30px;
}

input#email {
  background-position: 3px -30px;
}

textarea#comment {
  background-position: 3px -60px;
}
```

We can further enhance the form by adding a `:focus` state for active form elements. The CSS below changes the border to a soft blue color, and switches the grayscale icons out for a colored version. To do this, we simply swap the background's position:

---

[11] http://www.alistapart.com/articles/sprites

```
input:focus,
textarea:focus {
  border: 1px solid #26808c;
}

input#name:focus {
background-position: 3px -500px;
}

input#email:focus {
background-position: 3px -530px;
}

textarea#comment:focus {
background-position: 3px -560px;
}
```

Now you have colored icons, seen in Figure 4.11, when the field is active.

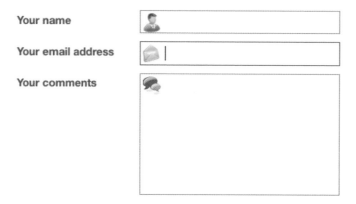

Figure 4.11. Our focused fields

The use of background images against text fields can make for some brilliant effects. Here's an example of how a grungy background can create the illusion of a rough, scruffy search box, seen in Figure 4.12.

Figure 4.12. A grungy search box

Daunting? Hardly! If you've been reading this chapter carefully, you already have the skills to make this a reality.

This design is lacking in a visible `label`, but we need to include that for reasons of accessibility, of course. Below is the markup we'll use for the form:

```
<form action="#" method="get" id="search">
  <fieldset>
    <!-- Search -->
    <div id="field-search">
      <label for="name">Search</label>
      <input type="text" name="search" id="search"/>
    </div>

    <!-- Controls -->
    <div class="controls">
      <input id="submit" name="submit" type="submit"
        value="Search"/>
    </div>
  </fieldset>
</form>
```

We can hide our `label` using a spot of absolute positioning to move the text far, far away from the edge of the screen:

```
div#field-search label {
  position: absolute;
  left: -999em;
  top: -999em;
}
```

The trick to creating the messy edges on the search field is to turn off all borders, add a grubby background image, and add some padding so that the text is still clear. Here's the CSS to work our magic on the search field:

```
div#field-search input {
  background: #fff url(css/images/bg-input-search.png)
  ➥no-repeat 0 0;
  border: none;
  display: block;
  float: left;
  font: 14px/1 "Helvetica Neue", Helvetica, Arial, sans-serif;
  float: left;
  padding: 6px 10px 7px;
  width: 243px;
}
```

You'll see that we've excluded a height declaration for this element. An important *gotcha* to remember when tackling this technique is that adding height to a text `input` element can yield unpredictable results across browsers; instead, simply apply padding to the top and bottom of the element until the text inside lines up to your taste. Using a `height` property for a `textarea` has no such issue, so there are no worries in applying some height to them to achieve the perfect layout.

There are many inventive, stylistic effects you can create with some judicious use of background images and borders. Go nuts, but remember that an effective form must still be usable and readable. Your hours of blood, sweat, and tears will be worth very little if your readers are unable to fill out the form easily.

Styling the Submit Button

So our users have made their way through a very nicely styled set of form questions—those users who are also fancy form aficionados may have even *oohed* and *aahed*—and are now making their way to the submit button. Then we'd best make sure that our submit buttons are fancy too!

Submit buttons can generally be styled in much the same way as text fields, allowing you to change the color, size, and font of text, as well as the borders and background color. However, this can become a little boring, and sooner or later you will find that you want to add some fanciness to those buttons. This will often call for image replacement, particularly when your desired font is Web unfriendly, or there are elements to the design such as rounded corners.

As mentioned earlier in this chapter, there are currently no CSS standards regarding how form widgets are styled, and our earlier image replacement techniques are no match for stubborn browsers. Luckily, some amazingly determined individuals in the Web development community have discovered an almost foolproof way of styling submit buttons.

This method works by removing some of the default browser styling from buttons, then setting a width and height for our button to match the size of the image we'd like to use, with the `overflow` property set to `hidden`. Next, throw in some padding on the top and left to match the height and width, and thanks to the `overflow: hidden` declaration, the text is pushed outside of the visible area. Finally, all we need to do is place the background image. Here's how that CSS could look:

```
input#submit {
  border: none;
  width: widthpx;
  height: heightpx;
  background: url(images/mybutton.png) no-repeat 0 0;
  margin: 0;
  overflow: hidden;
  padding: widthpx 0 0 heightpx;
}
```

 Camino Support: Missing in Action

This method is unsuitable if you need to support the Camino browser for the Mac. Camino is overly touchy about its buttons; it will correctly cause the text to disappear on the submit button, but will show no love for your background image.

Some other browsers—mostly older browsers—will simply ignore your styling and present a plain old button instead. That's quite okay, as this behavior means the button remains functional.

There's also a type of `input` element available to us, `image`. Much like a regular `img` element, you reference an image `input` like so:

```
<input type="image" src="images/submitbutton.png" alt="Submit"
  value="submit"/>
```

I bet you're wondering why we would tell you to use an image replacement here, instead of a nice reliable image? Well, I'm glad you asked.

The challenge with using an image as a button is that Firefox will send the button's value when the form is submitted, unlike Internet Explorer and Opera. It's possible to work around this with a spot of JavaScript or some clever server-side sniffing, but if you have a simple CSS-only way to deal with the issue, you can avoid all that. And of course, in the spirit of separating presentation and structure, we think that a spot of image replacement is the best solution. You can find an explanation of this issue at QuirksMode.[12]

What about the others?

Radio buttons, checkboxes, and buttons—where are they? We've avoided these deliberately; with CSS alone, styling any elements other than text inputs and textareas is fraught with peril. We'll learn about how a little JavaScript magic can pave the way for fancier select menus, checkboxes, and radio buttons in the next chapter. For now, we'll stick with simple styles like borders, spacing, and control over fonts.

For more information about the perils and limits of form element styling take a stroll over to Roger Johansson's excellent blog post, *Styling form controls with CSS, revisited*[13]—as well as discussing the pitfalls of trying to style certain kinds of form elements, it includes a whopping 224 screenshots of different browser and operating system combinations.

Putting It All Together

Let's put these techniques to the test by styling Fit and Awesome's Sign Up form. We've grabbed the Sign Up form's markup from Chapter 3, and placed it inside an HTML document. We've included our reset style sheet to tidy up any browser inconsistencies, and added a container `div` element for good measure—this will make it easy to perform some tricks later.

---

[12] http://www.quirksmode.org/bugreports/archives/2006/07/Namevalue_pairs_arent_submitted_for_image_submit_b.html
[13] http://www.456bereastreet.com/archive/200701/styling_form_controls_with_css_revisited/

Before we set up our design, let's see what our document looks like in a browser so far. In Figure 4.13, we can see our very plain form.

Sign Up

Already a member? Log in.

Hi there! We're excited to have you as a part of our community. To get started, please create an account.

Your email address [   ]
Create Password [   ]
Confirm Password [   ]
Your profile link fitandawesome.com/ [   ]
Birth date
Month [– Month – ▲▼]
Day [– Day – ▲▼]
Year [– Year – ▲▼]
This is hidden by default from your profile.
☐ I have read and agree to the Terms of Service.
(Create Profile)

Figure 4.13. Our vanilla form: ho-hum

Fancy? Hardly. Quick, let's create some visual structure, and add some light styling and typography. At this point, we can also add a `position` of `relative` to our containing `div` so that it's easy to move items about with absolute positioning:

ch04/css/fancyforms.css (excerpt)

```
html {
  background: #eee;
}

body {
  background: #eee url(images/bg-body.png);
  color: #333;
  font: 75%/1.3 "Helvetica Neue", Helvetica, Arial, sans-serif;
  padding: 20px;
}
```

```css
#container {
  background: url(images/bg-form-btm.png) no-repeat 100% 100%;
  padding-bottom: 18px;
  width: 600px;
  position: relative;
}

#container-inner {
  background: #fff url(images/bg-form.gif) repeat-x;
  border: 1px solid #fff;
  border-color: #fff #fff #ababab;
  padding: 20px;
}

a {
  text-decoration: none;
  color: #26808c;
}

a:hover,
a:focus {
  text-decoration: underline;
}

p {
  margin: 1em 0;
  padding: 0;
}

strong {
  font-weight: bold;
}

h1 {
  border-bottom: 1px solid #fff;
  background: url(images/bg-ccc.gif) 0 100% repeat-x;
  color: #666666;
  font-size: 2.5em;
  font-weight: normal;
  line-height: 1;
  margin: 0 0 0.7em;
  padding: 0 0 28px;
}
```

```
input,
textarea,
select {
  font-family: "Helvetica Neue", Helvetica, Arial, sans-serif;
}
```

Already, we can see an improvement to the legibility of our form. Figure 4.14 shows there's now a bit more room to breathe! We're in a good position to start layering on some fanciness.

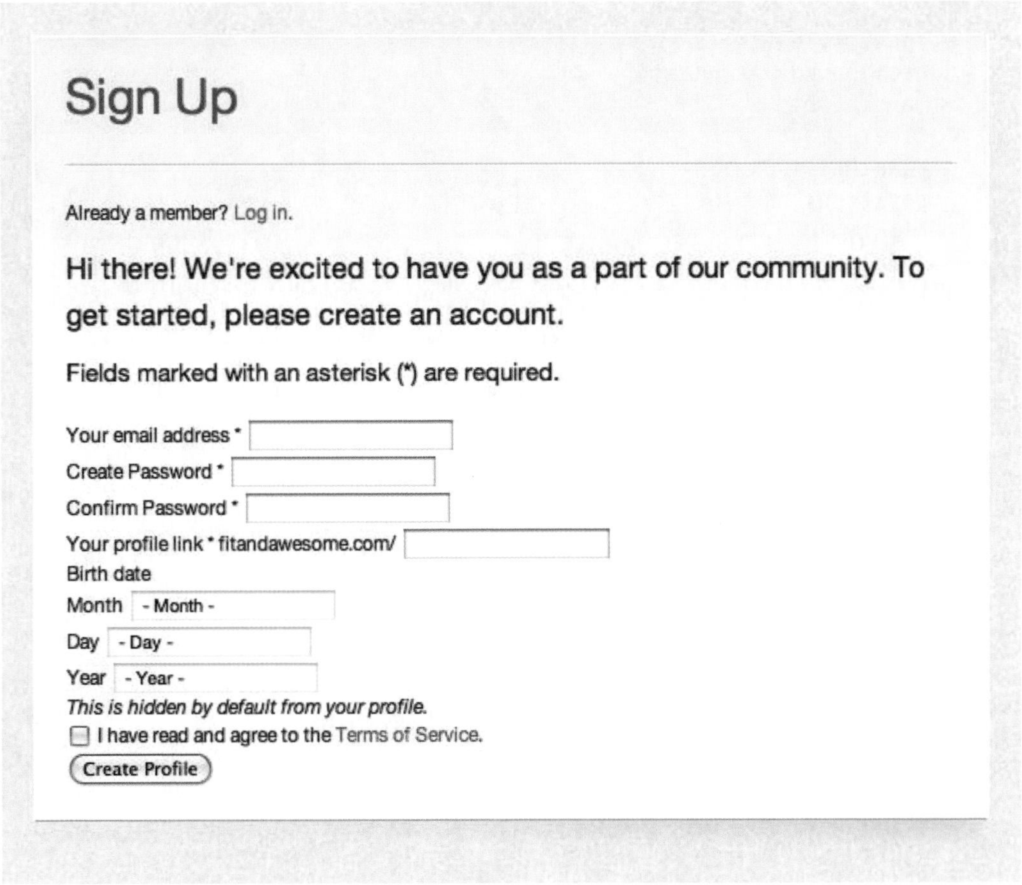

Figure 4.14. Better already!

The Login Link

Our design places the Login link text in the corner of the container, above the form's heading, but in the markup, the link actually sits below the heading. Moving that out of the introductory text is quite simple: add a little absolute positioning and background color, and that link moves up to the top right of our relatively positioned container `div`.

While we're thinking about the text at the top, we may as well style this as well:

ch04/css/fancyforms.css (excerpt)

```css
#sign-up .log-in {
  background: #eaeaea;
  margin: 0;
  line-height: 1;
  padding: 10px 12px;
  position: absolute;
  right: 20px;
  top: 30px;
}

#sign-up .log-in a {
  font-weight: bold;
}
  ⋮
.introduction {
  font-size: 1.5em;
  line-height: 1.6;
  margin: 0 0 2em;
}

p.note {
  font-size: 1.25em;
  margin: -1.7em 0 1.25em;
}
```

In Figure 4.15, we see what the top of our form looks like now.

Sign Up   Already a member? Log in.

Figure 4.15. Nearly there!

Aligning to the Grid

Our design makes good use of a grid to align fields and their labels. We'll start by
setting up the divisions which act as rows for our form. The `div` with the class
`controls` is the one which contains our submit button:

```
fieldset div {
  margin: 0 0 10px;
}

fieldset div.controls {
  margin: 25px 0 0;
  padding: 0;
}
```

Next, the labels. We'll float these to the left and give them a width, so that there's
room for the fields to settle to their right. While we're at it, let's add some typography:

```
                                          ch04/css/fancyforms.css (excerpt)
fieldset div label {
  color: #666;
  float: left;
  display: block;
  font-size: 1.16em;
  font-weight: bold;
  line-height: 1.1;
  margin: 7px 0 0 -160px;
  width: 140px;
}
```

As mentioned in Chapter 3, the asterisks that represent a required field sit inside
an abbreviation element, `abbr`, which must be positioned to the right of the field.

The asterisks are also significantly larger than they would ordinarily appear, so we'll add some text sizing to suit:

ch04/css/fancyforms.css *(excerpt)*

```
fieldset abbr {
  color: #7b0101;
  font-size: 20px;
  font-weight: bold;
  line-height: 1;
  padding: 0 1px;
  vertical-align: middle;
}

fieldset label abbr {
  display: block;
  font-size: 23px;
  padding: 0;
  position: absolute;
  top: 10px;
  right: 60px;
  width: 16px;
}
```

Our design calls for a nice amount of breathing room for our fields, so we'll specify some of these broadly by using a selector to grab all the inputs that are a child of a fieldset element, then overriding others to taste. The first input selector below specifies a width and padding, but for file upload features we'd like to avoid that. Instead, there's a CSS3 attribute selector to reset the width, padding, and border on file fields:[14]

ch04/css/fancyforms.css *(excerpt)*

```
fieldset div input,
fieldset div textarea,
fieldset div select {
  border-width: 1px;
  border-style: solid;
  border-color: #636d77 #a3b4c4 #c7d2de;
```

---

[14] Read all about attribute selectors at the SitePoint CSS Reference: http://reference.sitepoint.com/css/attributeselector

```
    color: #333;
    display: block;
    font-size: 14px;
    font-family: Arial, Helvetica, sans-serif;
    line-height: 1;
    margin: 0;
}

fieldset div input:focus,
fieldset div textarea:focus,
fieldset div select:focus {
    border-color: #636d77;
}

fieldset div input {
    padding: 6px 5px;
    width: 288px;
}

fieldset div select {
    padding: 0 0 0 3px;
    width: 291px;
}

fieldset div textarea {
    height: 89px;
    padding: 6px 5px;
    width: 288px;
}

fieldset div input[type=file] {
    background: none;
    border: inherit;
    padding: 0;
}
```

We will need to remove some of the styling on the inputs that are inside those unordered lists, though. Floating to the left and behaving like a block element is all very well when you're dealing with a nice big text field, but those little radio buttons and checkboxes should return to being inline. Since those elements will always be inside an unordered list, it's easy to target them with some descendant selectors:

```css
fieldset div ul {
  margin: 5px 0 0 0;
}

fieldset div ul li {
  margin: 0 0 5px;
  padding: 0;
}

fieldset div ul li label {
  display: inline;
  float: none;
  font-size: 1em;
  font-weight: normal;
  margin: 0;
  padding: 0;
}

fieldset div ul li input {
  background: none;
  border: none;
  display: inline;
  margin: 0 5px 0 0;
  padding: 0;
  width: auto;
}
```

Let's see how that turned out. In Figure 4.16, we're able to see that the inputs and labels are beginning to line up quite well in accordance with our design comp. All these styles are solid, generic styles that will suit all our forms. However, there are a few specific parts of this form that require their own particular styles. We'll look at these next.

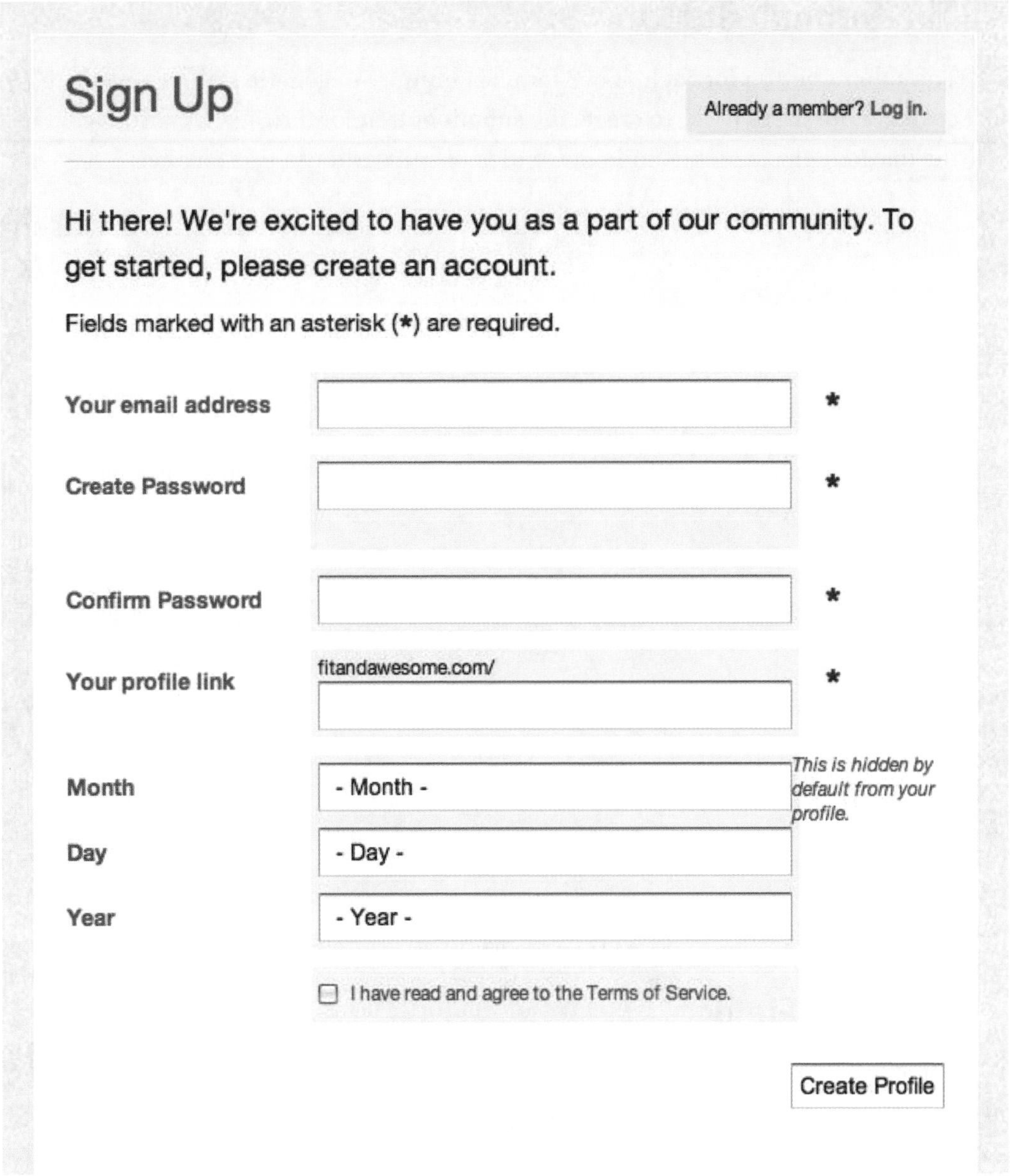

Sign Up

Already a member? Log in.

Hi there! We're excited to have you as a part of our community. To get started, please create an account.

Fields marked with an asterisk (*) are required.

Your email address   [   ]   *

Create Password   [   ]   *

Confirm Password   [   ]   *

Your profile link   fitandawesome.com/   *
                         [   ]

Month   [- Month -   ]   *This is hidden by
                                                   default from your
                                                   profile.

Day   [- Day -   ]

Year   [- Year -   ]

                         ☐ I have read and agree to the Terms of Service.

                                              [Create Profile]

Figure 4.16. More gridlike

The Submit Button

The submit button for each of our forms is unique—a generic style is unable to cover all our bases here. To create the submit button for the Sign Up form, we'll use the image replacement technique we discovered earlier in this chapter:

```
                                    ch04/css/fancyforms.css (excerpt)
input#submit {
  border: none;
  cursor: pointer;
  float: right;
  background: url(images/ir-submit-create-profile.png)
➥ no-repeat 0 0;
  width: 136px;
  height: 32px;
  margin: 0;
  overflow: hidden;
  padding: 32px 0 0 136px;
}
```

The result can be seen below, in Figure 4.17.

Figure 4.17. Our very own unique submit button

Prefixed Field

The field which requests your preferred address for your Fit and Awesome profile page is prefixed by the URL of the site. In the markup we have a span surrounding the URL, with a class of profile-link-prefix. We'll need to deal with those here:

```
                                      ch04/css/fancyforms.css (excerpt)

#field-profile-link .profile-link-prefix {
  display: block;
  float: left;
  font-size: 1.16em;
  line-height: 1.1;
  margin: 9px 10px 0 0;
  text-align: right;
  width: 133px;
}

#field-profile-link input {
  width: 145px;
}
```

Birth Date Fieldset

With our Birth Date question using three elements for one answer—year, month, and day—a little extra markup and styling prowess is required. The markup for these three select fields is wrapped with a fieldset and a legend combination. As we discovered in Chapter 3, the labels are required on each field to ensure that our form is accessible, adhering to best practice. The challenge is to make this set of elements blend in with the rest of the fields, as the design specifies. Here are the three tasks we'll need to undertake:

1. Make the surrounding fieldset's legend appear in the left-hand column, and style it like the other labels.
2. Hide the labels for the year, month, and day fields.
3. Adjust the widths and margins of each menu so they fit on one line.

In the following code we will do exactly that. Our fieldset to contain the date-of-birth fields has a class of group. We will adjust the margin for the date-of-birth section, then style the span inside the legend to resemble our other fields' labels, using selectors that target the group class:

ch04/css/fancyforms.css *(excerpt)*

```
fieldset fieldset.group {
  color: #666;
  margin: 0 0 10px 155px;
  padding: 0;
}

fieldset fieldset.group legend span {
  background: none;
  border: none;
  display: block;
  font-size: 1.16em;
  font-weight: bold;
  line-height: 1.1;
  margin: 9px 20px 0 -155px;
  padding: 0;
  position: absolute;
  left: 0;
  width: 140px;
}
```

select Widths and Internet Explorer 6

Internet Explorer 6 will lop off text in a select menu if the text within the options is wider than the width of the menu. It's possible to work around this with some JavaScript, but these can be a little tricky to make work. A more robust fix is to try and choose a width that would accommodate all those options.

Each of the three fields is contained within a div to help us out with positioning. We'll sit those divs next to each other, specify some appropriate widths, and then use some absolute positioning to place the labels far off the screen. To separate each field we'll also add a margin to the left of each div.

ch04/css/fancyforms.css *(excerpt)*

```
fieldset fieldset.group div {
  background: none;
  float: left;
  margin: 0 0 0 5px;
  padding-left: 0;
}
```

```
fieldset#section-dob div label {
  position: absolute;
  top: -999em;
}

fieldset#section-dob div select {
  width: 85px;
}

fieldset#section-dob div select#dob_month {
  width: 108px;
}
```

There's a note attached to the field that needs some attention as well. Using clear: left on the note will ensure it pops below the field, while a fat left margin will help us align it in the area to the right:

ch04/css/fancyforms.css (excerpt)

```
fieldset#section-dob em.note {
  clear: left;
  display: block;
  font-style: normal;
  margin: 0 0 0.5em 5px;
}
```

Figure 4.18 shows the result of the styles we just applied.

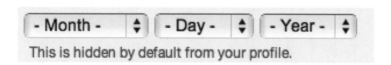

Figure 4.18. A vast improvement

The Final Touch

There's one last little touch—we need to include a soft gray background behind each field. There are a few different techniques we could use here: one could wrap each field or group of fields with a `div` to act as container element and set some padding and background color, or it might even be possible to use borders. However, it'd be extremely nice if we could avoid adding a bunch of presentational markup to the form.

A more robust option for our purposes today is to use a background image that contains white on the left and gray on the right, and apply that background to the `div`s that form each "row" of our forms. This will do a fairly good impression of resembling some well-constructed gray borders without adding even more elements to our markup. Let's give it a shot!

Here is the image in Photoshop that will be saved and repeated along the vertical axis.

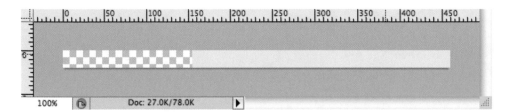

Figure 4.19. Our little background

We'll slip that in as a background image, and add some padding to create an effect that resembles a nice fat border:

```
                                ch04/css/fancyforms.css (excerpt)

fieldset div {
  ⋮
  background: url(images/bg-form-fieldset-div.png)
  ➥repeat-y 0 0;
  padding: 5px 5px 5px 0;
}

fieldset#section-dob {
  ⋮
  background: url(images/bg-form-fieldset-div.png)
  ➥repeat-y -155px 0;
  padding: 0;
}
```

The checkbox for the terms of service omits the gray background however, as does the div that contains the submit button. On top of that, the date fields should exclude the background image, otherwise the white at the left of the image will appear again and spoil the illusion! We'll override those like so:

```
                                ch04/css/fancyforms.css (excerpt)

#field-agree-tos {
  background: none;
}

fieldset#section-dob div {
  background: none;
}

fieldset div.controls {
  background: none;
}
```

Let's see how the final result, shown overleaf in Figure 4.20, turned out.

Sign Up

Already a member? Log in.

Hi there! We're excited to have you as a part of our community. To get started, please create an account.

Fields marked with an asterisk (*) are required.

Your email address [   ] *

Create Password [   ] *

Confirm Password [   ] *

Your profile link   fitandawesome.com/ [   ] *

Birth date   [- Month - ▾] [- Day - ▾] [- Year - ▾]
This is hidden by default from your profile.

☐ I have read and agree to the Terms of Service.

[CREATE PROFILE ▸]

Figure 4.20. That's fancy!

The techniques we've covered here should also provide you with the skills you need to complete most of the other forms. However, we have one outlier left to work on …

A Straggler: The Privacy Settings Form

The Privacy Settings form, as seen in Figure 4.21, breaks all the rules set by our other forms.

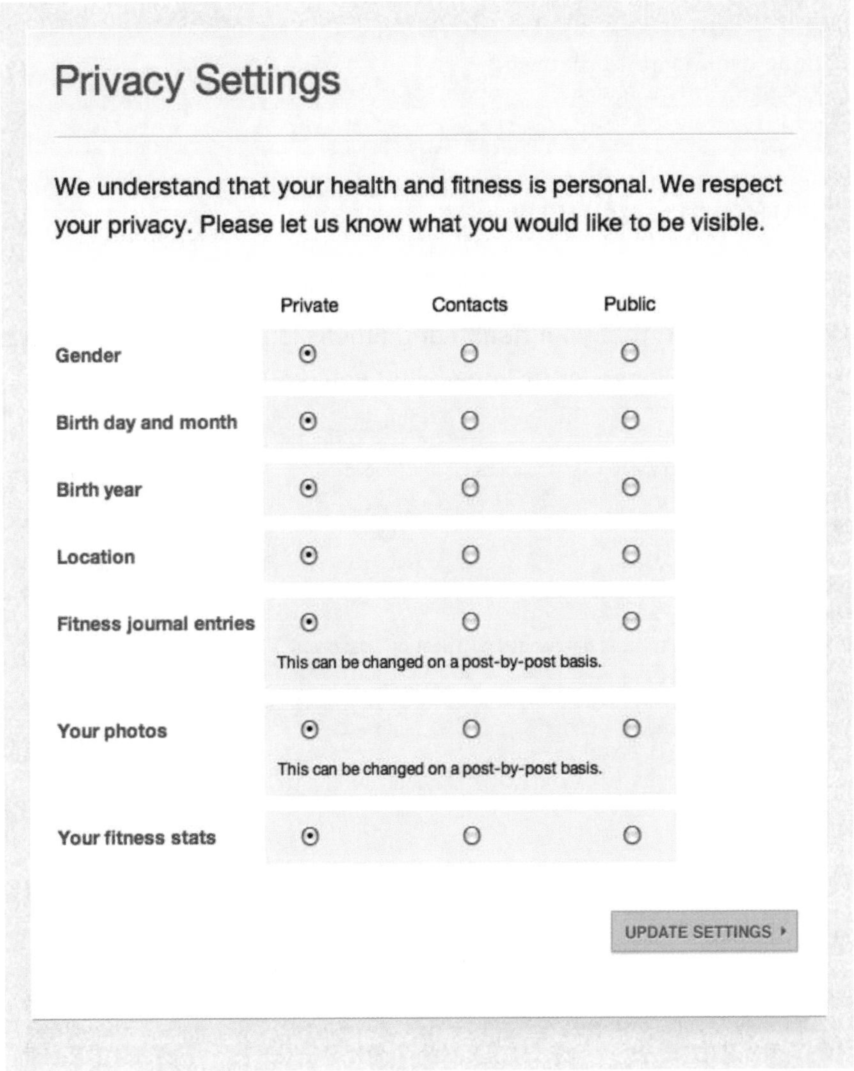

Figure 4.21. There's always one, isn't there?

This form is assembled with a semantic table of radio buttons. Our existing form styling has yet to cover the particular needs of this form, so let's add some more

CSS to account for this table. Instead of applying styling that directly styles the Privacy Settings table, we'll add a little extensibility to the mix by targeting tables and their components that appear within fieldsets.

Firstly, let's see what our table looks like before we begin. In Figure 4.22, we can see that we already have a bit of basic styling thanks to the CSS we added earlier, but the table itself is quite plain.

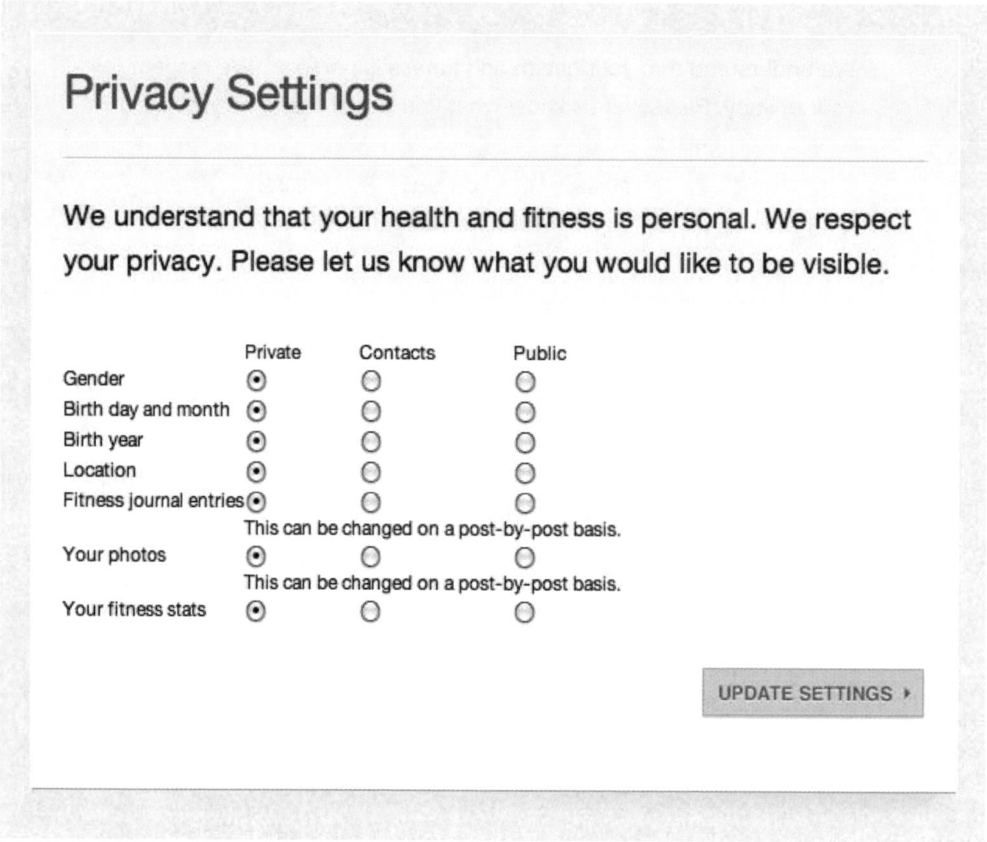

Figure 4.22. An unstyled privacy form

It's relatively quick and simple to add a bit more structure to that, however: some width takes care of that cramped feeling, while border-collapse and border-spacing declarations will eliminate any unwanted space between cells.

ch04/css/fancyforms.css (excerpt)

```
fieldset table {
  border-collapse: collapse;
  border-spacing: none;
  width: 465px;
}
```

Next, let's style the headings of our table to match the comp:

ch04/css/fancyforms.css (excerpt)

```
fieldset table thead th {
  color: #015;
  font-size: 1.16em;
  padding: 0 14px 8px;
}

fieldset table tbody th {
  color: #666;
  font-size: 1.16em;
  font-weight: bold;
  width: 155px;
}
```

A background, border and some padding on the table's cells will create the appropriate amount of space between each cell:

```css
fieldset td {
  background: #f2f2f2;
  padding: 12px 28px;
}

fieldset tbody th,
fieldset td {
  border: 10px solid #fff;
  border-width: 0 0 10px;
  vertical-align: middle;
}
```

All, that is, except the rows with a note, which should be smaller:

```css
fieldset tr.with-note td,
fieldset tr.with-note th {
  border: none;
}
```

All that is left for our table is to add a little polish by aligning each column evenly, adding a little padding to those notes, and making sure that the inputs inside the cells stop inheriting any margins or padding:

```css
fieldset th.private,
fieldset td.private {
  text-align: left;
}

fieldset th.contacts,
fieldset td.contacts {
  text-align: center;
}

fieldset th.public,
fieldset td.public {
  text-align: right;
}
```

```
fieldset td input {
  margin: 0;
  padding: 0;
}

fieldset td.note {
  padding: 2px 10px 12px;
}
```

Finally, we'll add the styling for the Submit button, in much the same way as we did in the Sign Up form. You'll find the finished article in the code archive.

Conclusion

Our forms are gradually becoming more like the lovely design we came up with back in Chapter 1. We've learned some useful techniques here to create a graceful and clutter-free interface from accessible, semantic markup. We've learned some important skills for accommodating the requirements of our design while keeping accessibility in mind.

Using the skills you've learned so far in this book, you should be ready to tackle a number of fancy form challenges. But to make our form truly fancy, we'll need to take it one step further: it's time to add some enhancements using JavaScript.

Chapter 5

Enhancing

Old-school Spider-Man fans will be able to tell you that with great power comes great responsibility.[1] This is especially true when it comes to enhancing an interface with the powerful tools of JavaScript.

JavaScript enables us to create beautiful visual effects, provide workarounds for older browsers' foibles, validate our users' input, and even submit the form without a new pageload—all wonderful additions to a truly fancy form. However, careless or inconsiderate use of JavaScript can actually make your form harder to use, or even completely unusable in some situations.

There are many examples of poorly implemented forms littered about the Web that *require* the use of JavaScript to conduct the simplest of tasks. Unfortunately this is to the detriment of those users without JavaScript support. Best practice, however, dictates that JavaScript should only be used as an enhancement for the underlying functionality provided by your markup and server-side scripts. When using Java-Script to enhance your form, it's beneficial to ask yourself the following questions: Is it worthwhile attempting to fill the form out with JavaScript turned off? Does

---

[1] *Amazing Fantasy #15* (New York: Marvel Comics, 1965)

each element still function? Will the scripts on your server still catch any problems with the form submission? You should able to answer these questions with a hearty *yes!*

For ease of learning and battle-tested robustness, this chapter will make use of the jQuery framework.[2] While it does add a little extra weight to your forms, the use of a JavaScript framework such as jQuery often proves to be faster than writing your own code from scratch and already features plenty of support for multiple browsers. Naturally, it's possible to write your own customized JavaScript to deliver the same enhancements or use a different JavaScript framework if you prefer. Whichever method you choose, this chapter should give you some solid ideas about ways to improve your forms.

Fancier Form Widgets

Chapter 4 revealed some helpful hints for styling elements within your forms. While text inputs, textareas, and submit buttons will accept styling from CSS alone, other elements such as select menus, radio buttons, and checkboxes will need a little more elbow grease.

Select Menu Styling

Once upon a time, if your web site included a select menu you were stuck with the native styling of each browser. Those days are nearing an end—the holy grail of select element styling is near. As frameworks like jQuery mature, more options for enhanced widget styling are popping up all over the place.

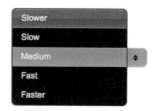

Figure 5.1. A glossy, colorful select menu

In general, these plugins work by creating a second widget that behaves as a proxy for the native select field. The native field is then made invisible, and all interactions with this proxy element are synchronized with the original select menu. Since the proxy is made of regular HTML elements, they can be styled quite easily.

---

[2] http://jquery.com/

Here are some of the menu styling jQuery plugins on offer out there:

- jQuery UI Selectmenu[3] is a jQuery UI[4] widget that throws in goodies such as icons, styled option text, and more. It's keyboard-accessible and comes bundled with multiple themes to use right away, though, of course, it's possible to create your very own styles.

  Since this plugin is dependent on jQuery UI, all of this appealing functionality does come at a price in the form of a hefty performance hit. This plugin is awfully hard to resist, though, with the promise of unlimited styling possibilities.

- A more lightweight alternative is a plugin called jQuery Custom Selectboxes.[5] This plugin's styling may require a little caressing before it looks stunning in all browsers, but these foibles are relatively easy to work around with some CSS prowess.

- Another smaller solution, the jQuery Selectbox plugin,[6] is well worth considering. This plugin is distinguished from other selectbox plugins by its extremely simple markup—styling this is a breeze.

Checkbox and radio button styling

JavaScript makes short work of CSS's limited support for checkbox and radio button styling. As with select menus, the usual practice here is to replace each native checkbox or radio widget with a proxy element; then utilize the magic of CSS sprites—such as those shown in Figure 5.2—to display beautiful customized widgets. In each state—normal, focused, selected, and selected with focus—the sprite is moved to its rightful place.

Figure 5.2. Radio and checkbox sprites

---

[3] http://wiki.jqueryui.com/Selectmenu

[4] http://jqueryui.com/

[5] http://info.wsisiz.edu.pl/~suszynsk/jQuery/demos/jquery-selectbox

[6] http://www.brainfault.com/2008/02/10/new-release-of-jquery-selectbox-replacement/

Here are a few plugins that will aid you in your quest for the perfect radio button:

1. The jQuery Custom Input plugin[7] by the Filament Group can deliver some very fancy radio buttons and checkboxes that are even keyboard-accessible. It works by wrapping each `input` and `label` pair in a `div`, providing an easy method for styling the entire item.

2. jQuery Geogoer VChecks[8] works in a similar fashion, adding classes to list items rather than `divs`. It's often a good idea to use list items for groups of checkboxes or radio buttons, so this plugin fits in nicely.

3. Many designers have been borrowing the iPhone's interface aesthetic and adding them to their sites. The jQuery iPhone-style Checkboxes plugin[9] converts your traditional checkboxes into modern, iPhone-style sliding switches.

Functional Enhancements

Of course, enhancements can be more than just aesthetic. Let's explore some of the functional enhancements that JavaScript can add to your forms.

Conditional Question Display

When there are multiple paths or questions dependent on other answers within a form, it's a good idea to only show those that are appropriate to the user. This helps speed up the form completion process, assisting the user by presenting just the relevant fields.

For instance, take an online store checkout page that offers a complementary gift wrapping option. Because it's an optional service, it makes sense to only show that field if the customer specifies that the purchase is a gift. Otherwise, we can omit it.

Here's some example markup for a fairly standard checkout page. We've eliminated much of the surrounding markup for brevity's sake, but you'll find a complete demonstration in the code archive:

---

[7] http://filamentgroup.com/lab/accessible_custom_designed_checkbox_radio_button_inputs_styled_css_jquery/

[8] http://vaziuojam.lt/js/geogoer/jquery_plugins/vchecks/index.html

[9] http://awardwinningfjords.com/2009/06/16/iphone-style-checkboxes.html

```html
<div>
  <ul>
    <li>
      <input type="checkbox" id="gift-wrapping" name="gift-wrapping"
        value="yes"/>
      <label for="gift-wrapping">
        This wine is a gift; please gift wrap for me
      </label>
    </li>
  </ul>
</div>

<fieldset id="section-gift-wrapping">
  <legend>Gift Wrapping Details</legend>
  <p class="note">If you would like gift wrapping,
    please fill out the following:</p>
  <div>
    <label class="heading">Box Type</label>
    <ul>
      <li>
        <input type="radio" id="gift-wrapping-type-wooden"
        name="gift-wrapping-type" value="wooden"/>
        <label for="gift-wrapping-type-wooden">
          Standard wooden case
        </label>
      </li>
      <li>
        <input type="radio" id="gift-wrapping-type-oak"
        name="gift-wrapping-type" value="oak"/>
        <label for="gift-wrapping-type-oak">
          Hand crafted oak box
        </label>
      </li>
      <li>
        <input type="radio" id="gift-wrapping-type-contemporary"
        name="gift-wrapping-type" value="contemporary"/>
        <label for="gift-wrapping-type-contemporary">
          Contemporary designer box by Ji Lu
        </label>
      </li>
    </ul>
    <div>
```

```
      <label for="gift-wrapping-message">
        Message
      </label>
      <textarea id="gift-wrapping-message"
        name="gift-wrapping-message">
      </textarea>
    </div>
  </div>
</fieldset>
```

 Stating the Obvious

You'll see that we included an introductory message at the top of the conditional sections. This is added to explain to the user why a section of the form has suddenly made itself visible. It also ensures that those users without JavaScript can still understand the purpose of the additional fields.

There are a couple of details we need to know about our form before we start our script:

1. What part of the form is the conditional section to be displayed?

2. What question will determine its display—the dependent field?

For the example above, the part of the form that will be conditionally displayed is the `fieldset` with an `id` of `section-gift-wrapping`. It'll be revealed when the checkbox titled `gift-wrapping` is checked. We'll kick off our JavaScript like so:

examples/gift-wrap.html (excerpt)

```
$(document).ready( function() {
  var conditionalSection = $('#section-gift-wrapping'),
  var dependentField = $('input[name=gift-wrapping]');
```

Next, we need to bind a function to the `change` event, so that when the checkbox is checked or unchecked, we can show or hide the section as appropriate. The first part of our `if` statement below applies when the appropriate radio button is checked; to be thorough, we also confirm the visibility of the conditional section. If that all pans out, we'll use jQuery's built-in `slideDown` effect to reveal the section in a graceful manner. Otherwise, we'll hide the section with the `slideUp` effect:

examples/gift-wrap.html *(excerpt)*

```
dependentField.bind('change', function() {
    if (dependentField.is(':checked') &&
    ➥conditionalSection.not(':visible')) {
        conditionalSection.slideDown();
        $(":input", conditionalSection).removeAttr("disabled");
    } else if (conditionalSection.is(':visible')) {
        conditionalSection.slideUp();
        $(":input", conditionalSection).attr("disabled", "disabled");
    }
});
```

We also want the conditional section to be hidden when the form is first loaded, so we'll trigger the above function as soon as the page loads:

examples/gift-wrap.html *(excerpt)*

```
dependentField.trigger('change');
```

Now, it's possible that a customer may fill out the gift field, then change their mind and decide to keep that gift for themselves! So, in the event that the customer unchecks that box, we should make sure that the gift fields are disabled. Failing to do so could mean that the values from these fields may be sent with the form once it's submitted, which may then result in some confusion. We'll add some lines to our if statement to add or remove the disabled attribute to the fields, as appropriate:

examples/gift-wrap.html *(excerpt)*

```
dependentField.bind('change', function() {
  if (dependentField.is(':checked') &&
    ➥conditionalSection.not(':visible')) {
    conditionalSection.slideDown();
    $(":input", conditionalSection).attr("disabled", "disabled");
  } else if (conditionalSection.is(':visible')) {
    conditionalSection.slideUp();
    $(":input", conditionalSection).removeAttr("disabled");
  }
});
```

Some browser testing at this stage will reveal that the change event in Internet Explorer is, of course, a little different to other browsers. Internet Explorer only initiates the `change` event when an input loses focus—a user would have to use the tab key or click another element before that section is revealed. In other browsers, the event occurs as soon as a change is made. To help IE, we'll fake that event by chaining a `blur` and `focus` event whenever a dependent field is clicked:

examples/gift-wrap.html *(excerpt)*

```
if ($.browser.msie) {
  $(dependentField).click(function() {
    dependentField.blur().focus();
  });
  var label = $("label[for=" + dependentField.attr("id") + "]");
  $(label).click(function() {
    dependentField.blur().focus();
  });
}
```

All is in working order. Upon loading the form, the gift wrapping section is hidden until the gift wrapping question is checked. You can see a working example, with all the code, in the code archive for this book.

Convert Your Work to a Plugin

One-off scripts like this are all very well when you only have one issue to overcome, but if your site makes repeated use of a particular technique, it's worth converting your work into a reusable jQuery plugin. You'll avoid having to write the same code over again, and if you release it to the world, you'll be helping other developers in the same boat! For more information on putting together a jQuery plugin, see the Learning jQuery site,[10] which is full of tutorials and book recommendations.

---

[10] http://www.learningjquery.com/

Date Selectors

Does your form request a date for an upcoming event or deadline? A date picker that's calendar-styled can work wonders, both for usability and for cleanly formatted data.

Figure 5.3. A date chooser created with jQuery UI Datepicker

Dates can be written a number of ways, which can be a little confusing at times. For example, 2nd October, 2010 could be written as 02/10/2010 or 10/02/2010, or if you're a fan of hyphens, 02-10-2010, and so on. Therefore, a mismatch between your expected format and a user's data is possible.

Many web applications may ask the user to choose a date far into the future or past, such as event calendars, flight booking services, or historical references. Have you ever tried figuring out what date Sunday six weeks from now is without the aid of a calendar?

Of course, you should try to encourage your users to enter the right format—Fit and Awesome's Sign Up and Profile forms use select menus to enforce the correct order. However, there's also a big usability benefit to be gained from choosing an intuitive widget.

jQuery UI's Datepicker,[11] shown in Figure 5.3, is highly customizable and easy to use. It does, however, come with a bit of additional bulk, since it relies on the jQuery UI library. However, it is packed with features that make it difficult to say no to—keyboard shortcuts to jump between months, plenty of ways to customize the output, and more.

---

[11] http://jqueryui.com/demos/datepicker/

If a jQuery UI-based solution is a bit too heavy for your liking, look no further than the lighter jQuery Datepicker plugin.[12] Confused by the similar names? It's because this plugin was actually the foundation for the UI plugin, but has since deviated down another path. Accordingly, many of the features are the same.

Password Strength Indicators

Password strength indicators have become quite the popular item in recent times. They're a good way to encourage your users to select passwords that are difficult to crack, which adds a layer of protection for you and your users against hackers. As more web sites include password strength indicators, the average user will be prompted to make their passwords more secure on a regular basis. In this situation, it's definitely a good idea to annoy your users somewhat.

While we're thinking about passwords, it's beneficial to help your users by providing a hint about how to make their passwords more secure. It's also ideal to inform them of any password strength requirements you may have, such as a minimum password length or whether it must comprise numerals and punctuation.

 A False Sense of Security

For a truly secure site, you'll need more than just a password strength indicator. Without encryption, password fields will be sent across the great divide as text that can be intercepted by shady characters.

If you're concerned about security—and you should be—always secure any Login and Sign Up forms with a security protocol such as Secure Sockets Layer (SSL). For more advice about the importance of securing information as it travels between your site and the user, read the article *Password Interception in a SSL/TLS Channel.*[13]

An example of an effective password strength indicator is the one Yahoo uses for its Sign Up form, shown in Figure 5.4. There's a note to explain minimum and maximum password lengths, an explanation of unacceptable passwords, and an indicator to show how strong the password is.

---

[12] http://keith-wood.name/datepick.html
[13] http://lasecwww.epfl.ch/memo/memo_ssl.shtml

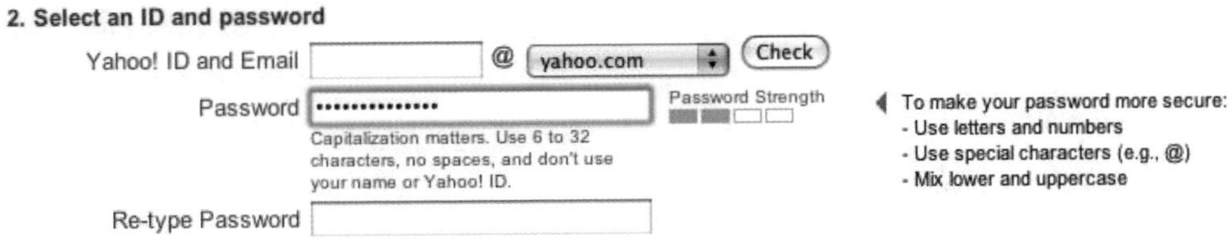

Figure 5.4. Yahoo's password strength indicator

■ PassRoids password strength plugin[14] provides easily styled output and a number of sensible features, such as checking two password fields to see if they match, offering instant feedback on an entered password, and even disabling the submit button if the password is unacceptable.

■ jQuery Password Strength Meter[15] can compare the value of the username field to a password, and present a message to the user if they match. This is a good way to discourage the common practice of using one's username as a password.

Autocomplete

As we learned back in Chapter 1, autocomplete fields are an efficient way to help your users choose from a number of options. They generally work by presenting a list of options as a user starts to enter text. As the user enters more text these options are usually filtered appropriately offering more relevant options to the user. A user should then be able to click the result that best matches.

Jörn Zaefferer's autocomplete plugin[16] is flexible, small, and highly configurable. It produces semantic markup full of design hooks, presenting autocompletion options within an unordered list.

Dylan Verheul's autocomplete plugin[17] is also easy to configure and light, with many of the same features and benefits of the above plugin.

---

[14] http://thecreativeoutfit.com/index.php?view=jQuery-Password-Plugin

[15] http://mypocket-technologies.com/jquery/password_strength/

[16] http://bassistance.de/jquery-plugins/jquery-plugin-autocomplete/

[17] http://dyve.net/jquery/?autocomplete

Input Validation

No matter how usable a form is, users are still likely to input invalid information, miss required fields, or misunderstand instructions. **Client-side validation** is a method of validating a form submission that's performed on the server and driven by JavaScript. The instant assistance and feedback helps users correct problems quickly, without waiting for the page to reload, and for the server to respond with the errors.

Validation is indispensable in ensuring that users enter required fields and provide information in the correct format. Here are a few key hints for validation to work at its best:

1. Let users know when they enter invalid information as soon as possible to give them the opportunity to fix things before they submit. If a user tries to select a username that's already taken, or their email address looks invalid, be kind and let them know straight away.
2. Provide the user with a summary of errors—if any—once the form has been submitted. A simple way to show this is to jump back up to the top of the form and indicate the number of errors, along with a friendly message. If you wish, you can go a step further, having each error within the list linking straight to the relevant field.
3. As we learned in Chapter 3, it's important to indicate invalid fields with more than one method. Combine text, color, and icons to cover all your bases.
4. As users correct errors, provide feedback to let them know that they're now fixed. Replacing grumpy error icons and red text with a friendly tick provides positive reinforcement and will make for one happy user.

By following these practices you can limit frustrating experiences for users and help them complete forms in less time. For more information on best practice for usability and accessibility, read the W3C's Web Content Accessibility Guidelines (WCAG) about how to minimize errors.[18]

---

[18] http://www.w3.org/WAI/WCAG20/quickref/20080430/

Server-side Validation is Still Necessary

We've said it before and we'll say it again: it's impossible to rely completely on JavaScript-driven functionality. You should ensure that the applications or scripts on your server will still perform the same function.

How can we add this to our forms? Since we're concentrating on jQuery, enter the jQuery Validation plugin.[19] Robust, mature, and extensible, it's part of the daily arsenal of many a developer. The plugin checks for conditions such as whether a field is required, minimum or maximum character length, valid number ranges, email formats, dates, and more. There's a cornucopia of validation methods—take a look at the validation plugin documentation for the complete collection. It's even possible to write custom methods with which you can perform your own validation checks.

Submission with Ajax

Have you ever wanted to allow a form to be submitted without refreshing the entire page? Doing so can work wonders for forms that appear outside a main content area, such as a blog's comment form, a contact function stashed in the footer of a page, or a poll that appears within a side column—visitors can perform these activities without leaving the page. We'll do this using **Ajax**, a set of technologies and techniques for developing interfaces and functionality that more closely resemble the smooth experience of a desktop application.[20]

The Fit and Awesome feedback form is the ideal candidate for this treatment. Since we're using jQuery, it's easy for us to submit it using the built-in `post`. From reading the documentation for the `post` function we need to pass three parameters:

- `url`—the URL of the page to load
- `data`—an object containing all of the form fields' values
- `callback`—a function to be executed once the form has been submitted

---

[19] http://bassistance.de/jquery-plugins/jquery-plugin-validation/

[20] Find out more about Ajax at the article which started it all, *Ajax: A New Approach to Web Applications*, by Jesse James Garrett, at http://www.adaptivepath.com/ideas/essays/archives/000385.php

The example code below binds a function to the submit event of the feedback form. On submit this function will call jQuery's post function, which submits the form to a simple PHP script called feedback.php. Once submitted, the function will replace the contents form with a message to say thank-you:

```
$("form").bind('submit', function() {
  var form = $(this),
    fields = {
      name : $('#name', form).val(),
      email : $('#email', form).val(),
      comment : $('#comment', form).val()
    },
    successMessage = '<h2>Thank You</h2>
    ➥<p>Thank you for your feedback! We appreciate it, and
    ➥will get back to you shortly!</p>';

  $.post(
    "feedback.php",
    fields,
    function() {
      form.replaceWith(successMessage);
    }
  );
  return false;
});
```

The post function works nicely for simple forms like a feedback form, but falls short of accounting for all errors, such as time out. If you do need to consider this and other server-side errors you may want to use jQuery's Ajax function, which allows you to specify an action to take if this type of error is encountered.

Back to Our Forms

We've explored a number of fun options for JavaScript enhancement. Now, let's see how we can apply these to our Fit and Awesome forms!

For now, we'll concentrate on our Sign Up form, since it's the one we're most familiar with from previous examples.

Enter jQuery

Since we'll be using jQuery, we'll need to add it to our code.

First, download a version of jQuery[21]—if you're working from the code archive, you'll find it in the js folder. Then, reference it in the head of your HTML document, like so:

```
<script type="text/javascript" src="js/jquery-1.3.2.min.js">
</script>
```

Cloud-hosted Frameworks

An alternative way to include jQuery in your projects is to use Google's Ajax Libraries API,[22] which serves up the latest version of jQuery and other libraries from Google's speedy servers. You can find out more about the process from the documentation.

The next step is to create a new JavaScript file, which we'll call init.js., to contain our declarations. We'll reference that in the head of our document like so:

```
<script type="text/javascript" src="js/init.js"></script>
```

Password Strength Indicator

Like most sites, Fit and Awesome requires a username and password for any user accounts. As the web site contains confidential information about the user, a password strength indicator would go a long way to encouraging users to make their accounts more secure.

The first step is to include and initiate the password strength plugin. For this example, we'll use the PassRoids plugin[23] discussed earlier—it's light and easy to use.

---

[21] http://jquery.com
[22] http://code.google.com/apis/ajaxlibs/
[23] http://thecreativeoutfit.com/index.php?view=jQuery-Password-Plugin

It's a waste of resources to fire up the plugin on every page when only one page has the form. The jQuery `getScript` function allows us to choose to only call the plugin when the Sign Up form, identified by `sign-up`, is present. We determine this through the use of jQuery's `size` function, which returns the number of elements in the document that have this `id`:

ch05/js/init.js *(excerpt)*

```
$(document).ready(function() {
  if ($('#sign-up').size()) {
    $.getScript(
      'js/jquery.passroids.min.js',
      function() {
        $('form').passroids({
          main : "#password"
        });
      }
    );
  }
});
```

The default output feels a little plain for our form, so let's add some sparkle by including a sliding password meter. Four CSS sprites, shown in Figure 5.5, symbolize four levels of strength.

This will be applied as a background image for each strength level. We'll also output a text message so that this indicator makes sense without color.

While the output of the PassRoids plugin is nice and simple, we'll require a little extra markup for truly fancy styling. Looking through the plugin, we can find a line that outputs a string wrapped with a span:

Figure 5.5. Four levels of strength

```
jQuery('#psr_score').html('Strength: <span class=psr_'
➥+levels[strength]+'>'+levels[strength]+'</span>');
```

Inserting an additional `strong` element to this string provides emphasis. We'll also wrap the span around the entire string:

```
jQuery('#psr_score').html('<span class="psr_'
➥+levels[strength] + '"><strong>Strength:</strong> '
➥+ levels[strength] + '</span>');
```

Now, all we need is to style the span. Below, we set a background image against all four possible password strengths and reposition the image to reveal the appropriate sprite:

ch05/css/fancyforms.css *(excerpt)*

```
#psr_score {
  background: transparent;
  display: block;
  margin: 0;
  padding: 0;
  width: 200px;
}

.psr_Weak,
.psr_Medium,
.psr_Strong,
.psr_Excellent {
  background: transparent url(images/bg-password-strength.png)
  ➥no-repeat 0 0;
  display: block;
  margin: 0.5em 0 0.2em 5px;
  padding: 10px 0 0;
}

.psr_Medium {
  background-position: 0 -50px;
}

.psr_Strong {
  background-position: 0 -100px;
}
```

```
.psr_Excellent {
  background-position: 0 -150px;
}
```

Your password fields should now be informing your users about their password choices. Figure 5.6 shows the end result!

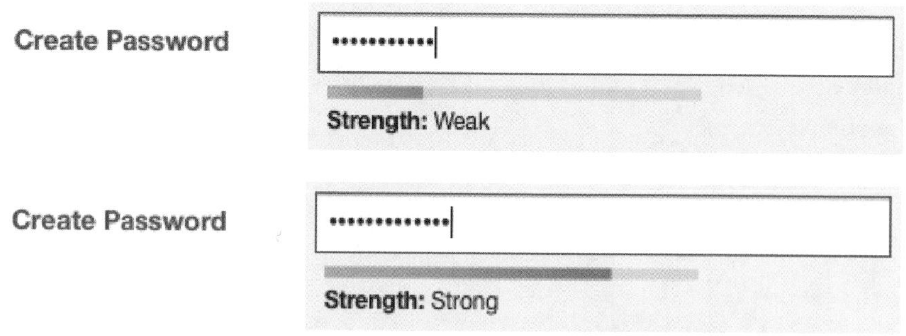

Figure 5.6. Our password strength indicator showing some muscle

Input Validation

We'll turn to jQuery's validation plugin and set up some rules for our fields. The method of doing so is quite straightforward; it looks lengthy, but it's reasonably easy to read.

We would like to validate the input when the user submits the form, and display the errors in an unordered list above the group of fields. Each error item will be a link to the appropriate field, so that it is easy to jump to the place where the error occurred.

As the user corrects the errors, we'll remove the red highlight from the troublesome field, delete the item from the list of errors, and replace the error icon with a tick to reassure them that it's correct. This is quite a lot of work, but the end result will be well worth it!

We'll start with our initialization block, in which we set up the rules for each field:

ch05/js/init.js *(excerpt)*

```
$('#sign-up form').validate({
  rules : {
    'email' : {
      required : true,
      email: true
    },

    'password' : {
      required : true
    },

    'password_confirmation' : {
      required : true,
      equalTo : '#password'
    },

    'profile_link' : {
      required : true
    },

    'agree_tos' : {
      required : true
    }
  },
```

Next, we'll continue this block with the messages to be shown whenever a field is missed. `email` and `password_confirmation` have additional display messages if the field contains content that's incorrect. Finally, we'll close the initialization block:

```
  messages : {
    'email' : {
      required : 'Enter your email address',
      email : 'Enter a valid email address,
      ➥for example user@example.com'
    },
    'password' : {
      required : 'Ensure your passwords match'
    },
    'password_confirmation' : {
      required : 'Confirm your password',
      equalTo : 'Ensure your passwords match'
    },
    'profile_link' : {
      required : 'Enter a link for your profile'
    },
    'agree_tos' : {
      required : 'You must agree to the terms of service'
    }
  }
});
```

Now, we'll override the plugin's defaults to more closely reflect our own needs. The code to perform this action begins by defining the elements we'll use to construct the list of problems, and then specifying the name of the class we'll use for highlighting a problematic field:

```
jQuery.validator.setDefaults({
  errorElement : 'a',
  wrapper : 'li',
  errorLabelContainer : '#form-messages ul',
  errorClass : 'error',
  focusInvalid: false,
  onfocusout: false,
```

We need to define what will happen when the plugin highlights the fields. In this case, we're appending an error icon to the content of the label that relates to the field. If an image with a class of `icon` is already there, we'll replace that with our error icon. Finally, we'll add a class to the field, `error`, which will produce our highlight:

ch05/js/init.js *(excerpt)*

```
highlight: function(element, errorClass) {
  var errorContainer = $(element).parents('div').eq(0);
  existingIcon = $('img.icon', errorContainer);

  if (existingIcon.size()) {
    existingIcon.replaceWith('<img src="images/icon-error.gif"
    ➥alt="error" class="icon"/>');
  } else {
    errorContainer.append('<img src="images/icon-error.gif"
    ➥alt="error" class="icon"/>');
  }

  $(element).addClass(errorClass);

},
```

When the user corrects a field, we'll remove the class and replace the error icon with an image of a green tick:

ch05/js/init.js *(excerpt)*

```
unhighlight: function(element, errorClass) {
  var errorContainer = $(element).parents('div').eq(0);

  if ($(':input.error', errorContainer).size() <= 1) {
    $('img.icon', errorContainer).replaceWith(
    ➥'<img src="images/icon-valid.gif" alt="Valid"
    ➥class="icon"/>');
  }

  $(element).removeClass(errorClass);
},
```

The next challenge is to populate the list of errors. Each error is linked to the appropriate field, so that it's easy to click and jump there.

We start by checking if there's already an error container on the page, and counting the number of errors we received. If there are any errors, we'll add our error message to the inside of the container. If the error message exists but there are no longer any errors, we'll update the container with a friendly message to inform the user that everything is now in order:

ch05/js/init.js (excerpt)

```
showErrors: function(errorMap, errorList) {
  var numErrors = this.numberOfInvalids();

  this.defaultShowErrors();

  if (!$('h2', errorContainer).size()) {
    errorContainer.prepend('<h2></h2>');
  }
  if (numErrors) {
    $('h2', errorContainer).html('<strong>Oops!</strong>
    ➥Your form contains ' + numErrors + " error" +
    ➥((numErrors == 1) ? '' : 's') + ':');
    $(this.currentForm).removeClass('valid');
  } else {
    $('h2', errorContainer).text('All errors have been corrected,
    ➥please continue');
    $(this.currentForm).addClass('valid');
  }
}
```

Fine so far!

Now to construct each of the links. When clicked, the links will scroll smoothly to the problematic field:

```
$('a', errorContainer).each( function() {
  var el = $(this),
    fieldID = el.attr('htmlfor'),
    field = $('#' + fieldID);

  el.attr('href', '#' + fieldID);

  el.bind('click', function() {
    field.trigger('focus');
    $('html,body').animate(
      {scrollTop: field.offset().top - 20}, 100
    );
    return false;
  });
});
},
```

A submit handler is dropped in to deal with a successful submission. Since we're playing with an example here, this simply displays a message:

```
submitHandler: function(form) {
  $(form).hide();
  $('<p class="introduction">Thank you for signing up.
  ➥Please check your email for further instructions.</p>')
    .insertBefore(form)
    .show();
  $('html,body').animate(
    {scrollTop: $("div#form-messages").offset().top}, 1000
  );
}
```

What's left? We still need to place that error container above our form, and reveal it when an invalid submission occurs:

ch05/js/init.js

```
var errorContainer = $('<div id="form-messages"><ul>
➡</ul></div>').hide();
errorContainer.insertBefore('fieldset div:first');

// Bind event to invalid form submission
$("form").bind("invalid-form.validate", function(e, validator) {
  errorContainer.show();
  $('html,body').animate(
    {scrollTop: errorContainer.offset().top - 20}, 100
  );

  errorContainer.focus();
});
```

That should be just about it! You can test out the final result in your code archive.

Select Menu Styling

As it stands, our Sign Up form is almost pixel perfect when compared to the original comp designed in Chapter 2. The only task left is to style the select menu widget according to the design.

So far we've managed to avoid using the hefty jQuery UI core or any of its plugins across our forms, and it'd be nice to keep our script overhead low—so let's bring in the jQuery Selectbox plugin.[24]

To ensure that we only load our plugin when it's needed, we'll turn to `size` and `getScript` again. This time, we're testing for the presence of any `select` element that's a descendant of a form element, and loading the appropriate plugin. Then, the `selectbox` function works its magic on every `select` we find:

---

[24] http://www.brainfault.com/2008/02/10/new-release-of-jquery-selectbox-replacement/

ch05/js/init.js *(excerpt)*

```
if ($('form select').size()) {
  $.getScript(
    'js/jquery.selectbox.min.js',
      function() {
        $('select').selectbox();
      }
    );
}
```

The plugin's default styling would suit our design quite nicely if the menus in our design had square edges. But alas, our design instead sports some lovely rounded corners. The simplest way of creating rounded corners with maximum cross-browser compatibility is to use the sliding doors technique.

The **sliding doors technique** places a large background image on the element you want styled, and on its parent element. Just like a sliding door, one of those images is aligned to the left and the other to the right. As the width of the element increases, the background of the parent element will slide out from underneath its child, which creates the optical illusion of a flexible background image.

One large background image that's positioned to the left or right will suffice: you'll see that in Figure 5.7.

Figure 5.7. One long menu background image

To employ the sliding doors technique an additional parent element is required. Rather than hacking the plugin or adding more markup to our HTML, we'll just have jQuery do it for us. We'll add that instruction to init.js:

```
                                              ch05/js/init.js (excerpt)

if ($('form select').size()) {
  $.getScript(
    'js/jquery.selectbox.min.js',
    function() {
      $('select').selectbox();
      $('input.selectbox').each(function() {
        $(this).wrap('<span id="wrapper_' + $(this).attr('id') +
        ➥'" class="selectbox-input-wrapper"></span>');
      });
    }
  );
}
```

Since the CSS provided with the plugin is already close to what we want, we can
create a new version based on it that includes a sliding door background image.
The plugin replaces each regular menu with a div, which will contain the unordered
list that presents the items. A class is added to the item that's selected and the item
that's currently beneath the mouse. Let's style these elements first:

```
                                         ch05/css/fancyforms.css (excerpt)

div.selectbox-wrapper {
  border: 1px solid #ccc;
  background: #fff;
  float: none;
  margin: 0 0 0 5px;
  max-height: 150px;
  overflow: auto;
  padding: 0;
  position: absolute;
  width: auto;
  z-index: 100;
}

div.selectbox-wrapper ul {
  background: #fff;
  float: none;
  list-style-type: none;
  margin: 0px;
  padding: 0px;
}
```

```
div.selectbox-wrapper ul li {
  cursor: pointer;
  display: block;
  list-style-type: none;
  margin: 0;
  padding: 2px 5px;
}

div.selectbox-wrapper ul li.selected {
  background-color: #EAF2FB;
}

div.selectbox-wrapper ul li.current {
  background-color: #CDD8E4;
}
```

Now to add the sliding door effect. The CSS to add the background to our select box and wrapper is shown below:

ch05/css/fancyforms.css (excerpt)

```
.selectbox-input-wrapper {
  background: url(images/ui-form-select.png) no-repeat 0 0;
  display: block;
  margin: 0 5px 0 0;
  padding: 0 0 0 10px;
  width: 293px;
}

.selectbox {
  background: url(images/ui-form-select.png) no-repeat 100% 0;
  border: none;
  display: block;
  margin: 0 -5px 0 0;
  padding: 5px 0;
  cursor: pointer;
  width : 288px;
}
```

Because we have some specific styles for the date-of-birth positioning, we had to update them to accommodate our desired layout.

Now our styling, shown in Figure 5.8, matches the original comp.

Figure 5.8. Our completed select menu style

Other Forms

You'll find complete examples of each form in the code archive, along with the JavaScript and source files. Feel free to use these as a basis for your own experiments. Pull them apart, pick out the juicy bits, mash them back together.

Beware, however, of adding too much eye candy. While we all love a little *ooh* and *ahh* in our lives, there's a fine line between graceful, groovy enhancement and outright annoyance. Use these newfound tools wisely, and you'll be sure to wow your visitors while ensuring a smooth, easy experience.

Conclusion

By now, you should be well-armed with the tools needed to create a variety of forms. We've covered the process of building beautiful, functional, well-structured forms, from the very first ideas all the way through to designing, building, and enhancing. Along the way, we've covered the tips, tricks, and gotchas that comprise the fine art of fancy form creation.

But there's more to do. With your forms ready for action, you're now able to start showing them off to the world. Your first step should be to observe your users and look for feedback. Conduct usability testing, run customer surveys, roll out your betas and demos, and then refine your forms again. As you do, you'll gain invaluable knowledge about how your users respond to your efforts.

And what of the other forms Fit and Awesome will need? How will users enter journal entries, record a new personal best, or plan out a training schedule? Well—we think that if you've been reading this book carefully, you'll already know how to answer that question. You now have all the tools to plan and build these. But better yet, we hope that you're ready to start putting these skills into practice on your own forms. We'll just have to wait to see what you come up with!

Index

BUILD YOUR OWN
WEB SITE
THE RIGHT WAY
USING HTML & CSS

BY IAN LLOYD
2ND EDITION

START BUILDING WEB SITES LIKE A PRO!

THE PRINCIPLES OF
BEAUTIFUL
WEB DESIGN
BY JASON BEAIRD

THE ART & SCIENCE OF CSS

BY **CAMERON ADAMS**
JINA BOLTON
DAVID JOHNSON
STEVE SMITH
JONATHAN SNOOK

CREATE INSPIRATIONAL STANDARDS-BASED WEB DESIGN

SIMPLY
JAVASCRIPT

BY KEVIN YANK
& CAMERON ADAMS

SIMPLY
SQL

BY RUDY LIMEBACK

THE FUN AND EASY WAY TO LEARN BEST-PRACTICE SQL

THE PHP ANTHOLOGY
101 ESSENTIAL TIPS, TRICKS & HACKS

BY **DAVEY SHAFIK**
MATTHEW WEIER O'PHINNEY
LIGAYA TURMELLE
HARRY FUECKS
BEN BALBO
2ND EDITION

SOLUTIONS TO THE MOST COMMON PROGRAMMING PROBLEMS

FANCY FORM DESIGN

CD-ROM

The CD-ROM is not missing.
Download all the code in this book from:
`http://www.sitepoint.com/books/forms1/code.php`